Daily Bread

A Handbook for Priests
Learning to Cook for Themselves

Tim Schoenbachler

Foreword by Rev. J. Ronald Knott

SOPHRONISMOS PRESS • LOUISVILLE, KY

DAILY BREAD
A Handbook for Priests Learning to Cook for Themselves

Contact information:
Daily Bread
2612 Frankfort Ave.
Louisville, KY 40206
EMAIL: dailybreadbook@gmail.com

Cover photos courtesy of Saint Meinrad Archabbey.
Thanks to Reverend William Schmid for allowing the use of his image.
Thanks to Rev. J. Ronald Knott for his encouragement and support in pursuit of this project.

First Printing: September 2014

ISBN 978-0-9858001-6-1

If you have any questions regarding the contents of this book or recipes herein or want to share some insights you may contact me via email at: **dailybreadbook@gmail.com.**

If you would like an **eBook version for your Kindle, tablet or iPad** email me an image/copy of your purchase receipt and I will send you a link to download it.

DEDICATION

To my parents, Anne and Forrest,
who nourished me in every way possible

and

to all of those who eat alone and
who take the time to prepare something
satisfying, healthy and delicious to eat.

TABLE OF CONTENTS

NOTE: Recipes that are underlined take 30 minutes or less. Those recipes with an asterisk take 30 minutes or less if you have leftover cooked meat or chicken.

APPENDIX

FOREWORD

On this mountain, the Lord of hosts will provide for all peoples a feast of rich food and choice wines, juicy, rich food and pure, choice wines.
ISAIAH 25:6

When I was Saint Meinrad Seminary's Director of the Institute for Priests and Presbyterates, I led the development of programs for those transitioning out of the seminary, those becoming pastors for the first time, international priests acclimating to American culture and seasoned pastors living alone. One thing became obvious – many did not know how to cook simple healthy meals for themselves.

Some, of course, were gourmet cooks, but the majority did not know how to eat healthily, much less prepare meals for themselves. Most priests today live alone without traditional housekeepers who used to do the shopping, cook meals and even serve it to them at regular hours. Many priests today eat on the run, often eating carry out or fast food late in the evening after a very busy day.

When this became a painfully obvious reality for those of us who developed the Institute for Priests and Presbyrates programs, I began to talk about the need for a "teaching kitchen" at the seminary. I talked about my dream of building such a kitchen to as many people as I could. Finally, a good friend of mine by the name of Jim Patterson II stepped up to the plate and helped me move it from a mere dream to a concrete reality.

The new "teaching kitchen" (see backcover photo), a dining room, a cozy gathering space and wet bar are a part of what has become known as the Saint John Vianney Center at Saint Meinrad. These spaces are used by program attendees for prayer, hospitality and education in ongoing formation programs which sometimes include cooking classes. This state-of-the-art "teaching kitchen" is comprised of a 12 seat, u-shaped counter built around two, four-burner cooktops where priests can observe and interact with a chef up close and have a hands-on experience. (A special thanks to Chef Kevin Maloney, Production Chef at *Volare Italian Ristorante* in Louisville, for his guidance and equipment donations while setting up the Teaching Kitchen.)

Some of the cooking classes have featured *hors oeuvres* for sporting events like the Superbowl, seal-a-meals, ethnic cooking, multiple meals from one chicken, American holiday foods and general healthy meals that are easy to prepare.

To augment the "teaching kitchen," it has been a dream to have a special cookbook for priests which explains in detail the basic things a non-cook should know about cooking and making simple, healthy meals for himself. We made an attempt several years back, but with this cookbook we have seen yet another dream come true for the Institute for Priests and Presbyterates. We thank Mr. Timothy Schoenbachler for producing this extremely useful tool for helping priests in today's church nourish themselves in healthier ways and become even more effective in their ministries.

Rev. J Ronald Knott
Founding Director, Institute for Priests and Presbyterates
August 4, 2014
Feast of Saint John Vianney

Cooking 101

This is my invariable advice to people: Learn how to cook — try new recipes, learn from your mistakes, be fearless, and above all have fun!

JULIA CHILD

This is a cooking book. It's not just about recipes, but about everything involved in cooking for yourself or others. There is **general information** about cuts of meat, seafood and vegetables — things you should know when you are grocery shopping or planning a meal. You need to have the right **cooking tools and equipment** and your **pantry** needs to be stocked with the basics you use almost everyday so you are not running to the market to buy something at the last minute. I have included lists of these items so you can stock your kitchen with the tools and items you need to prepare a meal. Because this book is targeted to single men I have reduced recipes to a single serving or double serving (for leftovers) where possible.

The recipes in this book offer a good smattering of the basic and most common comfort meals. Recipes for a stir-fry or enchiladas and some pasta dishes are so flexible because you can use meat, poultry, pork or shrimp.

You will see a circular marker on many recipes. These are a quick reference to the amount of time

to prep and cook the recipe. 30 means 30 minutes or less, 60 means 60 minutes or less. An "L" over 30 or 60 means 30 or 60 minutes if using leftovers like precooked chicken or beef. An "L" over an "S" means "low-and-slow" which applies to meats that require cooking 3 hours or more on a low temperature. Recipes that take 30 minutes or less are also **underlined** in the Table of Contents. Try to use them on a nights when you are short on time. If you know you will be around home for the day that's a good time to do a low-and-slow recipe.

Reading a recipe: Always read through a recipe and be sure you understand it before you begin so you have a general idea of what you will be doing.

Always read the notes under the recipe title. There are important tips and ideas about the recipe.

A meat thermometer is a MUST for every cook. It will prevent you from undercooking or overcooking your food. Make sure you have one.

The first thing you should always do when preparing a meal is to get out all of the ingredients, tools, mixing bowls and pots and pans you will need and have them ready on your countertop and stovetop. This makes the process less hectic.

Salt your food. Season your food and taste it during the cooking process. You will use less salt if you add it during cooking rather than at the end. Each time you add a new element to a dish give it a bit of salt. Always salt the water used to boil or steam vegetables and pasta.

Don't cook cold fish and meat. Let it come to room temperature before cooking otherwise the outside gets done long before the inside. The larger the item the longer it will take to come to room temperature. Depending on the size it may take from 10 to 30 minutes.

Deciding what to cook is always a problem. I often ask myself, "What am I in the mood for?" Nothing sounds "good." I find that if I **plan a week of menus in advance** it helps me avoid this problem. I have some "go-to" recipes that are simple that I can eat almost anytime, no matter my mood, that I can make in a pinch when I don't have time to cook something that might take a few hours of braising in the oven or on top of the stove.

I keep a list on my refrigerator door of the meats, poultry and seafood I have in the freezer as well as leftovers so I immediately know what I can prepare for a supper, what I might need to thaw for a meal or what I need to get at the market if I don't have it. Planning in advance allows me to create a shopping list for the week to pick up items I don't keep in the pantry or I am out of.

I try to vary what I cook for supper: chicken two or 3 times a week, seafood at least once a week, meat or pork a couple of times a week. See *A Week of Meals* in the Appendix.

What do you like to eat? What are your favorite meals? What do you know how to cook? What would you like to learn to cook? Write them down in the **Things I Know How to Cook** section on page 157. The internet is a great place to find recipes for foods you want to know how to prepare. Just *google* it and you will find countless recipes. *YouTube.com* has thousands of instructional videos showing you how to cook a host of things and cooking techniques like how to pound a chicken breast into a cutlet.

I am a big believer in leftovers. About half of the meals I cook I create a second serving that I can eat in a day or two or freeze for when I want it or need it. Always **label your leftovers** in the freezer with name and date. Even in clear containers a tomato sauce looks a lot like chili. Toss out anything that is over 3 months old. While the food may be safe to eat by that time the taste and quality have suffered.

Some things I always make in big batches like stewed chicken because I can freeze it in portions and use it in recipes without having to cook up a single piece of chicken. If I am frying a chicken cutlet I might fry two and freeze the second so I can chop it up for another recipe. I never make a small pot of chili or meatballs or spaghetti sauce — I always make a double batch which means I have several meals in the freezer on those days I don't have the time or will to prepare something from scratch.

Invest in good food containers of various sizes for use in the refrigerator and freezer. There is much discussion about the chemical BPA used in many plastic products and fears of it seeping into foods over time or especially when food is heated in the containers. Avoid containers marked with a recycle code or 3 or 7. Best to look for containers that state they are BPA-free. Remove foods from plastic containers and reheat them on a plate covered loosely with plastic wrap marked microwave-safe .

Time can be an issue with cooking. Your schedule may be quite erratic or full and recipes that require long cooking times might not suit your life-style. Sometimes I will prepare recipes first thing in the morning so at night I am already prepared. Sometimes if I am just reheating leftovers I will use the time to make something for the next day. Some recipes need to marinate or refrigerate for a few or several hours. These can always be done in the morning or the night before. I am always thinking ahead about what I will probably cook the next day. This way I can can do some pre-prep if I have the time. You also need to plan ahead if you need to **thaw out something that is frozen.** The best way is always to put the frozen item in the refrigerator the night before and let it thaw slowly. If something happens and you can't cook it the next day it will keep another day, but if you thaw something on the counter or in cool water and don't use it right away you should pitch it. It's not worth the consequences. You can thaw items in a microwave, but you must be careful. I do not recommend thawing meat, poultry or fish in a microwave. See *Thawing Meats Safely* in the Appendix.

If you want to cook a recipe in this book using a Crock-Pot, slow cooker or pressure cooker that does not state that it is for preparation in that type of appliance you often may do so. Look for a similar recipe in the cookbook that likely came with the appliance. Or look for the particular item you are cooking as used in a recipe in the book. If you want to cook a recipe with round steak, chicken, pork chops, etc., look for a recipe that uses that cut in the book. You may need to use less or more liquid depending on the appliance. The amount of time it takes to cook will be a major difference using these appliances. (*See more information on these types of cookers below.*)

Recipe substitutions: You may want to make a recipe, but discover you are missing an ingredient and don't want to run to the market. Decide if you think it is integral to the flavor. If not, make it without it. Example: Marsala wine is used in Chicken Marsala. It is integral to the flavor. Chicken broth can always be substituted for white wine and beef broth for red wine. If there is something in a recipe you do not like, go ahead and make it without it. Maybe you dislike green pepper. While it is important to the flavor of dishes in which it is used you can omit it. Use red or yellow bell pepper instead if you like them - they are more mild in flavor and sweeter than a green pepper.

Cleaning up: If there is a "bad" side to cooking it's the mess you make; some dishes require more pots and pans than others. I try to wash a bowl, plate, pot or pan as soon as I am done using it if I have time. I have a dishwasher, but I find I end up needing things I put in there before I get a full load. That's one of the "hazards" of being single. And worse, I hate starting to cook a meal with a sink full of dirty dishes from previous meals so I always make sure I start with a clean slate.

Conventional and Convection ovens: Many ovens today offer a convection cooking setting. Convection ovens have a fan which circulates the heat. In a conventional oven the heat just sits there. It can lead to uneven cooking. You shouldn't use the convection setting for everything you cook. It works best for things like roasts, cookies, cakes — anything you cook on a low-sided pan or dish. Don't use the convection setting for anything in a high-sided dish like a casserole, a covered dish or something covered in aluminum foil. Convection cooking takes less time so you have to adjust roasting and baking times. You can even set the temperature 25 degrees lower, but experiment to know how yours ultimately works. Convection works especially well if you are cooking more than one thing in the oven at a time.

Oven Temperatures: The actual internal oven temperature may be hotter or cooler than what you set it at. This will effect cooking times. You really never know if your oven is heating to the the correct temperature unless you test it. It's a good idea to do this. You can buy a thermometer that hangs on an oven rack permanently. Just watch it the next time you use your oven to bake or roast something that takes at least an hour. Check it a few times during the cooking process. Ovens typically heat a little higher than the initial setting and then cool below it before it reheats so there is an average temperature. Once you know you can adjust the settings for any future baking or roasting. There are other methods to test the temperature without a thermometer - just *google: How to test your oven temperature without a thermometer.*

Microwave Ovens: I can't think of one thing I cook in a microwave except a potato or popcorn. Microwaves cook by agitating the food's molecules. Agitated molecules create heat as they bump into one another. So it cooks at the molecular level. All other methods cooks by radiant from the outside in. Microwaves do serious damage to bread. Ever notice how tough it makes bread if you reheat it. If I need to thaw out some bread I might use a microwave for 10 seconds only. The residual heat will thaw it in a few minutes. Microwaves don't really brown foods like an oven or skillet either. Microwaves are great for reheating leftovers, but have you noticed how the center of the food is never as hot as the outer edges even in a microwave with a motorized turntable? I have found that you need to cook the food on high in 1 minute increments with a resting period of 2 to 3 minutes in between. This gives the heat time to distribute throughout the food or reheat them on a low power setting for a longer period of time.

Crock-Pots and slow-cookers: A government agency that regulates these appliances has changed the requirements for the temperature settings. The low setting, the temperature at which everything cooked on older models, was 200°F, but now it is 250°F, and the warm setting which was around 165 °F is now 212°F — the boiling point. With these changes slow cookers are no longer so slow. Many people are complaining that the contents of their slow-cookers are boiling even on the low setting which misses the whole point of slow cooking and simmering. You will have to read your manual regarding cooking times for foods since there is no standard while both old and new slow-cookers are out there. If you were planning on buying a slow-cooker I recommend you buy an electric roaster oven (not toaster oven). They look like a larger crock-pot, but more rectangular. These tend to give you a fuller and more adjustable range of cooking temperatures. You can even roast a whole chicken in them. They are designed for slow-cooking as well so look for one that has a temperature range that starts at 200 °F.

Pressure Cookers: Pressure cookers do what their name implies — cook under extreme pressure so what might take 3 hours in an oven or 8 hours in a slow-cooker may take only 45 minutes in a pressure cooker. They cook with very little water thus intensifying flavor. They are especially good at tenderizing tougher cuts of meat. There are stove-top models and electric models. You will pay from $70 to $300 depending on brand and model. If you buy one get one that is at least an 8 quart. Better to have one that is wider than taller which allows for more surface area for browning meat when that is called for before cooking. If I had to choose between buying a slow-cooker or a pressure cooker, the pressure cooker wins. Some pressure cookers makers claim you can cook an entire meal— meat, starch and vegetables — all at the same time. Impossible. Many vegetables turn to mush in the time it takes to cook a chicken.

Iron Skillets and Iron Grill Pans: There is probably no skillet material that is more versatile than iron. When an iron skillet gets hot it stays hot unlike other materials that quickly loose heat when cold food is added to them. Iron is the best material for deep frying if you don't have a deep-fryer unit. Iron also heats more evenly than other materials. Iron makes the best hamburgers indoors. Iron grill pans have become very popular as they mimic the kind of sear marks you get when grilling outdoors. The downside of iron is caring for it. First, a new skillet must be "seasoned" if the label does not say that it has already been done so at the factory. After use you never, ever let it sit in water or use soap and it must be dried thoroughly after cleaning. Information for care and cleaning should accompany the product or it can be found on the internet.

The PANTRY

If you keep the following items in your pantry and fridge you will have what you need on hand to make many dishes. Some brand names are given only as an example - most, not all, store equivalent brands are just as good. If your pantry is bare it makes cooking frustrating because you never have what you need.

IN YOUR SPICE RACK

table salt
ground pepper
Pepper corns if you have a pepper mill

Dried Spices: (toss after they are 1 year old!)
caraway seed
cayenne
celery seed
chili powder
cinnamon (ground)
cumin (ground)
dill
garlic powder (avoid garlic salt)
ginger (ground)
mustard (dry, ground)
nutmeg (buy whole seeds and store in a small container - use a microplane to grate)
onion powder
oregano
paprika
red pepper flakes
thyme
parsley (don't waste your money on flavorless dried parsley. Buy fresh curly leaf or flat-leaf and freeze in a freezer bag; snip off and chop what you need as you need it)

PANTRY STAPLES
Grouped according to a typical grocery aisle where related items are placed.

PRODUCE:

onions - yellow (if you do not cook often, store in the fridge or a cool, dark place)
potatoes - Idaho or russet or red potatoes (see info about potatoes on page 126 to determine which type you will use most often) - if watching your starches, buy red potatoes as they are the lowest in starch. If you do not cook often, store in the fridge

vegetable bin or a cool, dark place.)
celery
carrots (whole - avoid pre-cut)
bell pepper - green or red (store in a container to prolong life)
lemons
garlic (keep it in the butter compartment)

DRY GOODS AND BAKING

rice - boil-in-bag or long grain white rice
boxed rice mixes for a quick side dish like - *Near East* brand Rice Pilaf and long grain and wild rice mix (like *Uncle Ben's*)

sugar
light brown sugar
honey

cornstarch
All-Purpose flour
Baking Powder
Baking Soda
Breadcrumbs
Bisquik or store brand equivalent (useful for making drop biscuits, pancakes, dumplings...)
cooking spray (like Pam)

apple cider vinegar
balsamic vinegar (*Pompeian* brand)
red wine vinegar (*Pompeian* brand)

canola oil
extra-virgin or virgin olive oil - used for salad dressings or low-temp cooking (sautéing). It has a low smoking point so should **not** be used for high temp cooking or frying.

CANNED GOODS

Tomatoes:
tomato sauce - a few small cans (8 oz.)
crushed tomatoes - a few cans (14 oz.)
diced tomatoes - a few cans (14oz.)
tomato paste - a few cans (6 and 12 oz.)

Soups and Broths:
cream of mushroom soup
canned chicken broth - low sodium
canned beef broth - low sodium
onion soup or beefy-onion soup mix (like *Lipton*)

Canned Vegetables:
canned green beans (if you can find **whole** canned green beans - not cut greens beans - they are much better)
canned new potatoes - whole
canned chili beans

crackers/saltines (regular or whole wheat)

tuna (canned)

Pasta:
spaghetti - vermicelli or angel hair
ziti or mini-penne
egg noodles

For Mexican dishes:
Taco Seasoning - mild or hot
Salsa Verde
chopped green chiles

STAPLES IN THE FRIDGE:

Condiments:
dijon or spicy brown mustard
ketchup
mayonnaise or Miracle Whip (your preference)
Worcestershire Sauce
Soy Sauce
Hot Sauce - *Tabasco* or equivalent
jam or jelly

Meats:
bacon *(if you don't eat bacon often, freeze it in small packages of 4 strips so it does not get old in the refrigerator)*
lunch meat for sandwiches

Dairy:
eggs
butter/margarine
milk
sour cream
cheeses: sharp cheddar, parmesan, mozzarella, swiss, American, Velveeta (makes very smooth and cheesy sauces)

IN THE FREEZER:

Vegetables:
frozen corn
frozen peas
frozen lima beans

Meats, Poultry, Seafood
keep items in your freezer you like and know you will cook like:

chicken - *keep a bag of frozen chicken cutlets or a package of split chicken breasts or thighs on hand.*
hamburger - *buy in 2 pound packages and split into 1/2 pound packages and freeze. It will thaw faster when needed.*
smoked sausage - *always a quick meal when needed*
pork chops or pork cutlets - *wrap in portions after purchase and freeze*
steak
shrimp - medium (41-50) or medium-large (36-40) uncooked, shelled and deveined

STORAGE AND BAKING

aluminum foil (regular and non-stick)
extra-wide aluminum foil
freezer bags (quart and gallon size)
plastic wrap
parchment paper

KITCHEN TOOLS

Here is a list of essential kitchen tools every cook needs to have at their disposal. Having the right tool for the job at hand makes cooking easier. The ones marked with a star I find extremely helpful. *Images are examples only, not an endorsement of any brand or style.*

Cutting Boards are one of the most "dangerous" kitchen tools as they can harbor food-born bacteria like ecoli. Traditional wood cutting boards are perhaps the worst offenders since wood is porous and absorbent. Tempered glass is a good board surface, but over time a lot of slicing and chopping can dull your knives because the surface is so hard. Read the label before you buy and look for words like - *antimicrobial, non-porous, non-absorbent, will not damage knives.* There are some woods that meet these specifications today. Also look for boards that have some kind of **non-slip** backing.

Knives: invest in good knives as they are you're most important tool. They are worth every penny. Knives that are not sharp will lead to kitchen accidents.

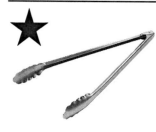			
STAINLESS STEEL MIXING BOWLS A set with lids. (Don't buy aluminum bowls as the metal reacts with salty and acidic foods.)	**GLASS MIXING BOWLS** A set with lids.	**SPATULAS** They come is regular and wide widths. Get one set in stainless steel and one set in silicone or other non-metal.	**LARGE SLOTTED SPOON** Get one in metal and one in non-metal.
★ 			★ 
LOCKING TONGS These are a must for every cook. Get 2 pair, one with and one without rubber tips.	**CUTTING BOARDS** It's good to have at least 2, one large and one small.	**SOUP LADLE**	**KITCHEN SHEARS** For cutting through bone, snipping herbs...

WHISKS
Get one medium or large metal and one non-metal. Use for beating eggs, mixes, egg whites, whipped cream...

DRY MEASURING CUPS
One set in metal. Stay away from plastic.

MEASURING SPOONS
One set. Stay away from plastic.

MEASURING CUPS
Get a 2 cup and a 4 cup - in glass.

SILICONE SPATULAS
Used for mixing. Get a couple.

MEAT MALLET
One version. Used to pound meat like chicken breasts into thin cutlets.

MEAT MALLET
Another version - this one also has a meat tenderizer side.

VEGETABLE PEELER
There are many styles.

MANDOLIN SLICER
This makes slicing and chopping easy. Look for ones that do several tasks and thicknesses.

MICROPLANE
THE tool for finely grating and zesting: lemon, garlic, parmesan cheese, etc.

WIRE MESH COLANDER

COLANDER
metal or plastic

FINE MESH STRAINER/SIFTER
Get one 3-1/2 inch diameter and one 6 inch to 8 inch diameter.

HAND MIXER
Get one that has attachments for mixing, kneading and whisking.

MEAT FORK
For stabilizing meat, chicken, turkey when carving.

SALAD SPINNER
For drying lettuces.

POTATO MASHER
For making mashed potatoes and mashing vegetables for other dishes.

FAT/GRAVY SEPARATOR
Makes it easy to separate meat fats and juices when making gravies. Get a 4 cup with a strainer top.

BOX GRATER
Each side has a different grating surface - for grating cheese, onion, carrot, etc.

BLENDER
Look for one that has enough power to crush ice.

MEAT THERMOMETERS (out of oven)
You must take the meat out of the oven, insert the probe and determine the internal temperature.

MEAT THERMOMETERS (in oven)
TOP: old-fashioned in-oven type. BOTTOM: a probe inserted in the meat with a long cord connected to a read-out that sits on the stove.

PASTRY BRUSH
Used for basting and spreading glazes.

CANDY/DEEP FRY THERMOMETER
A must-have if you deep-fry and you don't have a deep fryer appliance.

KITCHEN KNIVES

There are 4 knives that every cook needs. Cheap knives will not cut cleanly. They require more pressure when cutting and chopping which means more likelihood of slipping and cutting yourself. There is nothing more aggravating than trying to slice meat and the knife will not cut. Good knives are not cheap.

Expensive brands: Henckels, Shun, Wusthofs.
Well-rated but less expensive: Victorinox, Ginsu.

If you buy a set of knives, save your receipts. If they do not cut easily take them back!

Four essential knives (from top down)

CHEF'S KNIFE
most versatile knife in your kitchen, used for almost any chopping, slicing, trimming or carving. Usually the blade of a chef's knife is around 20cm (8") in length. Traditionally, the blade is curved to allow a rocking motion when chopping with a minimum of force.

BREAD KNIFE
You want a 10 to 12 inch blade. When cutting anything soft, the serrated edge makes it easy to cut into the object. Also works well with soft vegetables like tomatoes. You can find smaller serrated edge knives for that purpose as well.

UTILITY KNIFE
A smaller version of the chef's knife, typically with a 4 to 6 inch blade. The utility knife is used for chopping smaller items such as garlic, making shallow cuts or incisions, or creating cavities in a roast for garlic and herbs), and any cutting where greater control over a small area is required.

PAIRING KNIFE
A small knife with a blade about 3 to 4 inches long. It is commonly used in the preparation of fruit and vegetables, since the narrowness of the blade makes it easier to change direction mid-cut. It can be used to peel, to remove seeds and stalks, and to shape decorative shapes into fruit and vegetables.

BAKEWARE AND ROASTING PANS

The following are the essential pieces of cookware you need to properly furnish your kitchen. It is difficult to cook when you do not have the necessary equipment. Invest in quality products that will last.

Baking equipment is typically made of glass or aluminum and many of the aluminum pans come with a non-stick surface. **Stay away from dark-colored non-stick** as it tends to burn foods faster than the light grey pans.

Ceramic bakeware is a good investment. **Never pour cold water into or on a hot baking pan or dish.** It might break or warp it.

BAKING DISH
This is one of the most versatile of baking dishes. It may be glass or ceramic. Some come with a snap on lid.

Get 2: one, 9 inch by 13 inch and one, 9 inch by 9 inch.

PIE PLATE
You use this for pies (obviously) but it can be used for other things as well. Some are glass and some are ceramic.

Get at least one at least 9 inches round.

QUICHE/TART PAN
If you like to eat Quiche, this pan is designed for it although you can use a pie plate. You can also use this to make delicious fruit dessert tarts. Non-stick is good. And get one with a bottom that comes out.

BAKING DISHES
It's good to have a variety of ceramic baking dishes in various sizes for doing small or large casseroles.
Many are designed to go from "freezer to oven/microwave" without breaking.

MEATLOAF PAN
Designed to keep a meatloaf from cooking in its own fat drippings. Can also double as a bread pan without the insert or use to make a 2-serving lasagna.

BUNDT / TUBE PAN
Bundt cakes are one of the easiest cakes to make.
Non-stick is best.

BROILER PAN
Most all ovens come with this pan. Used for broiling meats like steaks, it allows fats to drip into the pan and not flare up in a fire. The bottom can be used as a shallow roasting pan.

SHEET PANS
Used for roasting, baking cookies, biscuits, etc. Have 2: 17-18 inches long, one non-stick and one metal. Use non-stick when doing cookies, biscuits, breads. Use metal when used for roasting.

ROASTING PAN For roasting a whole chicken, turkey, rib roast, pork loin. Hard anodized **with a rack insert** is best, about 13 inches by 16 inches.	**MUFFIN PAN** For muffins or cupcakes. Used also to make some *hors d'oeuvres*.	**SPRINGFORM PAN** If you make a cheesecake you really need this pan. It has a removable bottom.	**PIZZA PAN** The perforated pan helps the crust get crisper. Can double as a cooling rack for cookies.

*Do you know what breakfast cereal is made of? It's made of
all those little curly wooden shavings you find in pencil sharpeners!*
ROALD DAHL

COOKWARE: POTS AND PANS

A list of essential pots and pans every cook needs to have at their disposal. Having good quality cookware is important and having the right pot or pan makes cooking a lot easier.

Non-stick vs. stainless steel: Non-stick cookware has the advantage of easy release of foods and easy cleanup. It's great for foods like eggs, pancakes, dishes with cheese, sautéing vegetables, light pan-frying. **You do not want to use non-stick on a high heat** for things like searing meat or frying hamburger - you use a steel pan for that. **Steel pans clean up easily** if you know how - when you remove whatever you are cooking from the pan, remove the pan from the heat, pour in a little cold water, enough to cover the bottom about 1/8 inch. It should sizzle and steam. Wait about 10 seconds and scrape the bottom with a hard spatula. **DO BE CAREFUL:** if the pan is very hot the water can pop and spit. You can also just add some water to a pan that has cooled down and bring it to a boil for about a minute. **Aluminum pans** are OK if they are heavy. Thin aluminum pans are not. If you pick up a pot or pan and it weighs next-to-nothing - put it back. Good cookware has some weight.

The best pans have an encapsulated aluminimun disc on the bottom at least 3/8 inch thick.

NON-STICK FRYING PANS	**STAINLESS STEEL FRYING PANS**	**COVERED DEEP SKILLETS**

NON-STICK FRYING PANS

Used for sautéing, light frying.

If you buy cheap non-stick pans the surface will wear off and scratch in very little time despite what the label may say. Invest in a high-quality brand like *Cuisinart, Caphalon, Analon, Circulon.* Some department store chains (Macy's, Penny's, etc) will have their own brand that are similar to the high-end ones and are quite good. If it says "hard-anodized" that's good.

You will want at least 2: a **10 inch and a 12 inch.**

STAINLESS STEEL FRYING PANS

Used for sautéing, frying, searing, braising.

Look for a **.6mm stainless steel gauge** with **"encapsulated aluminum disc base."** When the pan gets hot it stays hot and distributes heat evenly. Do not waste your money on aluminum pans. Look for ones that can also be put into an oven

You will want at least 1, **12 inch.**

COVERED DEEP SKILLETS

Used for sautéing, braising, frying, stewing.

You will want at least 1, **12 inch** stainless steel, but I recommend a second one in non-stick.

DUTCH OVEN

Dutch Ovens are versatile pots that are used on the stovetop or in the oven to braise/stew dishes at low temperatures for a long time (low and slow) or cook in deep fat. They might be aluminum, ceramic, or perhaps the best known and **best type - enamel coated cast iron**. Pricey, but worth it.

You will want something in the **6 quart** range. It should not be non-stick, unless the coating is enamel or ceramic which have non-stick properties.

STOCK POT

Used for making large amounts of soups, stews, tomato sauces, boiling large amounts of pasta.

You will want something in the **6 to 8 quart** range. It can be non-stick or steel. Foods in steel will need more stirring as foods tend to stick on the bottom when cooked over a long period of time or if they are thick.

SAUCEPANS

Use for sautéing, boiling, steaming, braising small amounts.

Look for the anodized and steel varieties.

Get 2 each of non-stick and steel in size ranges: **1.5 - 2.5 quart** and **3.5 - 4 quart** size.

They come with options like glass lids, pouring spouts and straining lids - all good-to-have features.

SAUCEPAN WITH STEAMER INSERT

This is a handy pot when you want to steam vegetables like broccoli, asparagus, Brussels sprouts, etc.

STEAMER INSERT/BASKET

This is a handy gadget that you place in the bottom of a saucepan. It fans out to fit most small to medium saucepans. Add water and some salt just up to the bottom of the insert, place it in the pan and put your vegetables on top. Cover and steam.

UNIVERSAL POT/PAN COVER

This is handy when you want to cover a skillet that does not have a lid.

Buy a 12 inch or a size that will cover your largest non-lidded frying pan.

Bake: cooking with dry heat usually in a pre-heated oven.

Baste: moisten during cooking by applying a liquid, butter, or pan juices to keep the things from drying out or to add flavor. Use a spoon or brush.

Beat: mix rapidly with a spoon, fork, whisk or hand blender to make a smooth mixture.

Blanch: to boil in water for a brief amount of time to prepare something for another dish, set the color or seal in juices. Also a way to remove skins and shells.

Boil: to bring liquids to the point that they bubble rapidly. *Rolling Boil* — very intense bubbling; *gentle* or *medium boil* — between a rolling boil and a simmer.

Braise: to cook slowly in a covered pot with a little liquid; sometimes with aromatics and vegetables. Same as parboil.

Cream: to work a food or foods until creamy and blended, as in "to cream butter..."

Deglaze: to remove any burned-on bits (fond) that accumulate on the bottom of a pan after frying or sautéing; liquid is added to the hot pan and scraped up with a spatula or spoon. Sometimes the liquid is boiled down and reduced to make a glaze for the cooked meat or poultry or used to enrich a more complex sauce or gravy.

Drippings: the juices, fats and browned bits that collect in the bottom of a pan after something is roasted. These are often used to make a sauce or gravy.

Floret: broccoli and cauliflower are made up of stems and their florets — small groups of rounded sections.

Fold: to incorporate an aerated substance like whipped egg whites or cream into a thicker or heavier substance. Add 1/2 of the whipped element and with a spatula cut it into the center of the heavier substance by going under the substance and then out to the rim while folding it over on itself. Repeat this step while turning the bowl each time you mak a fold until it is incorporated. The point is to not stir it in which will deflate the whipped substance and cause the dish not to rise or be as fluffy as desired.

Fry: to brown and cook something in a a small anount or a shallow layer of fat, oil or butter or both on medium to medium-high heat. This is usually called pan frying. **Deep-fat frying** requires a deep, heavy pan with 3 to 4 cups of a frying substance like oil, shortening or lard. The frying temperature depends of the item being cooked. A deep-fat thermometer is normally used to dertermine when the fat is ready.

Julienne: to cut into thin strips

Parboil: precook in boiling water. Often done with potatoes to bring them to almost tender for a casserole.

Poach: simmer gently

Sauté: to cook on low to medium heat in a skillet or saucepan generally with a small amount of oil, butter or a combination of the 2. There should be just a hint a sizzle. This is not frying which requires a higher temperature and more oil.

Scald: refers to heating milk just to the point it begins to boil and then remove from the heat.

Score: make shallow cuts in meat or fish or the fat of a piece of meat or pork.

Sear: browning meat, pork, chicken on very high heat to seal in the juices and add flavor.

Simmer: to cook on low heat so that liquids are just slightly bubbling.

Whisk: using a whisk to beat a substance until well mixed

Zest: Special tools like a microplane or zester are used to finely grate the rind of citrus fruits like lemons, limes or oranges. Only the rind, the thickness of a sheet of paper, is used. The pith, the white part of the rind is not used.

CHOPPING AND SLICING

Practically everything you cook or make requires some chopping or slicing. While I have somewhat mastered the art of chopping I still use a **mandolin slicer** for many of those tasks especially if I have a lot of something to slice or chop.

If you have **good, sharp knives** chopping and dicing and mincing and slicing are much easier. A dull knife not only makes it harder, but more dangerous because as you try to force a dull knife through something it may slip instead. For some reason a dull knife may not cut through a tomato, but it will easily cut human flesh!

There are various terms which describe the size of a chopped or sliced item.

 **Chopped**: a generic term for cutting something up into small pieces; about 1/4 to 3/8 inch squarish.

Course Chopped: about 1/2 inch squarish pieces or 1/2 inch long pieces.

Rough Chopped: about 1 inch squarish pieces or 1 inch long pieces.

Diced or Fine Diced: chopping about 1/8 to 3/16 inch squarish pieces.

Minced: chopping something very tiny, about 1/16 inch squarish pieces. Usually for garlic or shallots.

CUTTING TERMS:

Chiffonade: stack the leaves (herbs, spinach, greens), roll tightly, then cut into thin , long strips.

Julienne: 1/8 inch by 2 to 3 inches long.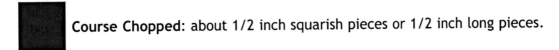

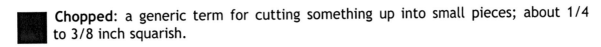

NOTE: It's easier and better to use a large knife to chop and slice. A small knife will work fine to slice up a carrot or some celery, but a large knife is called for when chopping something like onions. With a large knife you can get a rocking motion as you slice. Check out *YouTube.com.* for video demonstrations on the proper way to hold a knife and chop and slice.

SEARING

Many meat and chicken recipes call for searing the meat in advance of roasting like a tenderloin or beef roast. This has two purposes: it seals the exterior of the meat to help lock in its juices and it adds flavor the exterior of the meat.

Make sure the meat, pork, poultry, etc., is dry before you sear it. Pat it dry with a paper towel. If you marinated it be sure to pat it dry. Wet protein will not sear properly. Salt and pepper the protein just before you sear it. Salt will draw out moisture if you salt it and let it sit.

Never use a meat fork to lift or move or turn a piece of raw or searing meat. You are only making holes that allow its juices to run out. Use a pair of tongs.

The meat is normally salted and peppered and placed in a skillet or a Dutch Oven pot on medium-high to high heat with a little oil. The meat is turned and seared on all sides. **Leave it alone for a few minutes** once you put it in the pan and allow it to sear. If you try to move it and it resists then it has not seared. It you try and force it you will tear the meat.

Once the meat is seared on all sides you can place it on a roasting pan and roast it according to the recipe for temperature and time. If you are using a Dutch Oven you then add the ingredients given in the recipe, cover and either place in the oven or simmer it on the stovetop.

SLICING MEATS

There are certain cuts of meat that have lots of muscle fiber that require special care when slicing or they will be difficult to chew. **Beef brisket (and corned beef), flank steak, and flat iron steak** are the cuts that **must be sliced against the grain** to make them more tender. The grain in these cuts is fairly evident when you look at them — long parallel lines that resemble wood grain. These are muscle fibers. When you cut them across the grain you are shortening the length of the fiber thus making it easier to chew. There are muscle fibers in all meat, but depending on where they come from the cow they have more or less muscle fiber. Even a T-bone or rib-eye steak benefits from cutting against the grain though it has less fiber. On these steaks the muscle fiber runs parallel to the bone so cutting them crosswise to the bone makes every bite more tender.

MAKING A ROUX

A **roux** (roo) is a basic element in many recipes. A roux is used to make gravies, sauces, soups and fillings. It is what gives body and thickness to many dishes. It is one of the basics a cook needs to master. Once you make a roux a few times it's as easy as pie.

A roux has just **3 ingredients:**
some **fat** (butter or a meat fat or sometimes oil)
some **flour**
some **liquid** (broth or **cold** milk)

There are **general proportions for a roux:** for every 2 tablespoon of fat and flour you use 1 cup of liquid. This creates a mixture that will coat the back of a spoon - usually what you want in a gravy or sauce. Thicker gravies use more fat and flour or less liquid. The meat fat will come from cooking meat or poultry. It has to be separated from the juices. Using a gravy/fat separator is ideal for this. (See *Gravies*, page 28.)

Making a roux:

Start by melting the fat (butter or meat or poultry fat) in a saucepan on medium heat.

Stir in the flour with a wooden spoon or a whisk or small spatula — make sure you are using exact tablespoons, not more or less. A thin paste will form.

Cook it on medium heat for at least 2 minutes, stirring often. This cooks out the raw flour taste.

Sometimes you want a pale or white roux, but sometimes you want a dark roux. It depends on what the roux is for. A cheese sauce starts with a white roux. Soups start with a white roux. Creole dishes often use a dark roux. A hearty chicken or beef gravy uses a dark roux. To make a dark roux you keep cooking and stirring it until it becomes dark brown.

Once the desired color is reached slowly add your cold liquid while stirring briskly. Lumps should disappear as you stir. Further simmering will slightly thicken the mixture. The longer it simmers the thicker it will get. Normally you are looking for a consistency that will coat the back of spoon when you dip it in the sauce, hold it up and turn it sideways. The sauce shouldn't just run off, but a thin coat remains on the spoon.

Cheese sauce - add 1/2 cup or 1 cup grated cheddar or parmesan, gruyere or Swiss per 1 cup liquid to a butter and milk light roux after the liquid has been incorporated and simmered for a few minutes until thickened. Remove the pot from the heat and add cheese and constantly stir until melted. Add a dash of salt, pepper and fresh nutmeg.

BREADING AND FRYING

Many foods that you pan-fry, bake or deep fat fry are first dredged in flour or coated with a breading.

Dredging

Dredging involves some flour seasoned with salt and pepper and perhaps some other spices or herbs as suggested by the recipe. Flour and seasonings are put on a plate, in a bowl or perhaps a bag like in the case of oven-frying bone-in, skin-on chicken. Dredging something in flour protects the surface of the item from drying out and getting tough.

The food should be at room temperature, not cold. Be sure to use paper towel to pat dry the food you will be dredging. Whatever you dredge should be dry. If the piece of meat, chicken or fish is wet the flour becomes more like a paste and that is not what you want.

The item is slightly pressed into the flour on both sides until well coated. The excess is then shaken off and it is placed on a clean plate. It is always good to let the dredged item sit for at least 10 minutes before frying. Then it is placed in a pan that has some oil or a mixture of oil and butter that is on medium-high heat. The heat level is important. If the pan is not hot enough the coating will just sit in the oil and absorb it. Anything dredged in flour should only take a few minutes to brown. Toss a pinch of flour in the oil. If it sizzles quickly the oil should be hot enough to fry.

Thin cuts of chicken and pork or fish will normally be cooked through to doneness. Thicker cuts like cubed beef that will be used in a stew are not cooked through, just browned on all sides before it is added to another pot with other ingredients.

Breading

Breading is a little more complicated and messier. It usually involves a 3-step process. The 3-step process includes dredging in flour, dipping in a liquid and then coating in some type of crumb coating. It requires that you set up 3 "stations" for this process plus a clean plate onto which you place the breaded food.

The liquid is typically an egg wash — an egg beaten with a tablespoon of water or milk. Sometimes buttermilk is used in place of an egg wash.

The crumbs might be breadcrumbs, cracker crumbs, cornflake crumbs, panko breadcrumbs or even almonds that have been ground up. It might be a mixture of crumbs and parmesan cheese or almonds. You can buy different types of crumbs at the market or make them yourself in a blender or food processor. It's much cheaper to buy an inexpensive brand of plain cornflakes cereal and make cornflake crumbs yourself and store them in an airtight container. Or put your crackers or cornflakes in a plastic bag, seal and run a rolling pin or wine bottle over them until reduced to crumbs.

When you get your hands in flour and egg you can end up with a globby mess on your hands. There is a method to keep this from happening. You will use one hand as a "dry" hand and the other as a "wet" hand. First, set up your three breading stations — a shallow dish or bowl for flour, egg wash and crumbs. You can work from left to right or right to left depending on your preference. For this description we will work from right to left.

1. With your right hand (dry hand) dredge the item in the flour and shake off the excess flour.

2. Now place the item in the egg wash being careful not to let your fingers get wet.

3. Use your left hand (wet hand) to submerge both sides in the egg wash. Lift it above the container and let the excess egg drip off for 2 seconds and transfer it to the crumbs being careful not to touch the crumbs with your eggy fingers.

4. Now use your right hand (dry hand) to toss it or roll it in the crumbs, lightly patting the crumbs onto the surface. When done place it on a clean plate. When you are finished coating all the pieces you will be cooking put the plate in the fridge for 10 minutes.

You cannot reuse any flour or breadcrumbs that are leftover as they have touched raw food.

PAN-FRYING

The Skillet: If you are pan-frying one or two items use the smallest skillet that will hold both, but without crowing them. If you are frying several use your largest skillet. You may even need to pan-fry in batches keeping the fried items warm on a plate in the oven.

The Oil: You can pan-fry in plain oil — canola or olive oil (not extra-virgin) or a mixture of oil and butter. Butter has a low smoking point which means it will burn at a low temperature so it is not good for frying by itself. However, you can use oil and butter because the oil raises the smoke point of the butter. Some things you pan-fry require just a thin coat of oil like a thin chicken cutlet. A salmon patty or crab cake, because it is thicker, will require about 1/4 inch of oil.

The Heat: Your oil must be hot enough to fry. If it is not your coating will just soak up the oil and come off the meat and taste greasy. Put your oil in the pan and set the burner on medium-high heat. Watch the oil. When you see it start to shimmer, the surface of the oil begins to move in waves, your oil is ready. If it starts to smoke your pan is a little too hot. Just pull it off the burner for a minute. You can also **test the heat** by tossing in a pinch of flour or breadcrumbs. If they immediately sizzle your oil is ready.

When you place your dredged or battered food in the pan it should sizzle. If not, the pan is not hot enough. **If it starts to spit and pop** pull the pan off the heat for 30 seconds and reduce the heat to medium and return the pan to the burner.

Never move the item once you place it in the pan. Leave it alone for a few minutes. If you try to move it and it resists then it hasn't formed a crust yet. If you move it before it has formed a crust, the crust will stick to the pan and come away from the item. **Never use a fork to stab it and turn it** — use tongs or a spatula to turn. A fork will cause the juices to run out and create steam and steam will ruin a breading. When the edges of your item begin to look cooked, opaque or dry that is a clue that it is ready to flip. If you see juices in the food beginning to percolate to the top turn immediately. You don't want the top to get wet and ruin the coating.

Cooking Time: A breaded chicken cutlet or thin piece of fish will only take about 3 or 4 minutes a side on the right heat. That is enough time to brown the breading and cook it. A crab cake or a salmon patty may take about 4 to 5 minutes because you are not cooking the crab meat, just warming it. A thick piece of fish like a breaded piece of sea bass or cod will take about 5 minutes per side. Thicker cuts of meat or fish will take longer so you will need to adjust your heat so that it doesn't get too brown before it is time to flip it.

BAKING

Some things that are breaded (not just dredged) are baked, not pan-fried, like fish or baked chicken tenders. This is sometimes called oven frying. They are placed on a lightly greased pan and baked in a pre-heated oven at the temperature described by the recipe

GRAVIES

A gravy is a type of roux. There are simple ways to make a gravy and ones that take a little more time, but they have a lot more flavor. You can always buy dry gravy mixes or jar gravies at the market, but they are high in salt and chemicals. In a pinch, when you don't have meat juices, they will work. Generally you make a **scratch gravy** if you bake a whole chicken or turkey or a beef roast and have meat fats from the meat.

To make a **scratch gravy** you will need **all the juices** that are in the cooking pan - the broth and the fat. A **quick gravy** does not use the fat, **only the broth.**

Separating the broth from the fat:

Use a 2-cup or 4-cup glass measuring cup or gravy separator depending on how much liquid has been produced by the cooked poultry or beef.

When you have finished cooking your chicken or beef you will pour all of the juices into a glass measuring cup or ideally, a "gravy separator," a kitchen gadget that makes separating fat from liquid much easier. A worthy investment. (The spout comes from the bottom, so when you pour the liquid from the separator into a pot or bowl, the broth comes out first leaving the fat in the bottom.) If you use a measuring cup you need to place a **strainer over the cup** to catch bits of meat fat, herbs, etc. If your gravy separator doesn't have a built in strainer you will need to use one.

You will let the strained liquid sit in the measuring cup or gravy separator for at least 10 minutes so that the meat fats rise to the top as it cools. (Some people add a few ice cubes to hurry that process along. You can also put it in the freezer if you have space.) Once you see a definite layer separation of fat (usually a shiny, yellowish color) and liquid you may begin.

This recipe makes about 1 cup of gravy.

You will need 1 cup of broth and 2 tablespoons of fat for this recipe.
If you do not have enough broth from the cooked meat you can add some
low-sodium canned broth.

*You can freeze unused juices and fat for future gravies when your meat
or poultry doesn't produce much of either and you would like to make a gravy.*

If making a SCRATCH GRAVY you need:
   2 tablespoons of **flour,**
   2 tablespoons of **fat** and
   1 cup of **broth** - either the meat juices, the meat juices and some broth or all broth. (The
      ratio for making a scratch gravy is 2 tablespoons each of flour and fat to 1 cup or broth.)

If making a QUICK GRAVY you need:
   1 tablespoon of **cornstarch,**
   3 tablespoons of **cold water** and
   1 cup of **broth** - either the meat juices, meat juices and some broth or all broth.

SCRATCH GRAVY:

If you have poured the liquids into a **glass measuring cup** and are making a **scratch gravy,** spoon 2 tablespoons of the fat into a medium sauce pan. Be careful to get **only fat.** Any broth you remove with the fat makes a scratch gravy more difficult. Discard remaining fat or freeze for another use.

If using a **gravy separator, slowly** pour the broth in a measuring cup until you see the fat coming out. Stop and put the fat in a small bowl. Put 2 tablespoons of the fat into a medium sauce pan.

1. Add 2 tablespoons of flour to the fat, mix and cook on medium heat until it becomes the color of peanut butter or a little darker. This browning of the flour is what gives the gravy its intense flavor.

2. Now add about 1/4 cup of the broth while stirring constantly with a whisk or spatula until it becomes thick and smooth.

3. Add another 1/4 cup and do the same stirring it until there are no lumps.

4. Now add the rest of the broth and bring to a simmer and cook for a few minutes to thicken.

5. Taste it - it might need a bit of salt and pepper. If you want it thicker, cook it longer; thinner - add a little more broth.

6. Sometimes a little butter is stirred in at the end once you turn off the heat. It gives the gravy a silky shine and added richness.

QUICK GRAVY:

If you have poured the liquids into a **glass measuring cup** spoon off the fat and discard it or freeze it for a future time when you might want to make a scratch gravy.

If using a **gravy separator, slowly** pour the broth into a measuring cup until you begin to see a little of the fat in the pour. Stop and discard or freeze the fat.

Put **1 tablespoon of cornstarch** in a small bowl. **Add 3 tablespoons** of cold water. Mix well. This is called a *slurry*.

1. Pour 1 cup of the liquid into a small saucepan. Add broth if you don't have a cup of liquid from the meat.

2. Stir **one half of the slurry** into the broth in the saucepan. Bring it to a simmer. The liquid must be simmering for the cornstarch to thicken it. Let it simmer for 2 minutes.

3. If you want your gravy or sauce thicker stir in the rest of the cornstarch slurry and cook it for 2 more minutes.

4. If you accidentally get it too thick just add some more broth or water.

5. Sometimes a little butter is stirred in at the end once you turn off the heat. It gives the gravy a silky shine. Once you make a gravy this way a few times you will understand how it works!

CREAM GRAVIES

Cream gravy is what you typically find served over biscuits, mashed potatoes or something like chicken fried steak. It's also tasty on pork chops. Like all gravies it starts with some fat and some flour for a roux.

I have had cream gravies that were way too greasy. I could feel my veins clogging as I ate it! It all depends on how you make it. Sometimes a lot of meat or pork grease is used, but you can use very little and still get a lot of flavor.

Here are 2 versions: a simple cream gravy and a sausage gravy

SIMPLE CREAM GRAVY

INGREDIENTS:

Equal parts of oil or melted bacon fat and flour: 2 tablespoons of each will make about 1 cup of gravy. Bacon fat makes a tastier cream gravy.

1 cup of milk, salt and pepper.

DIRECTIONS:

(A whisk is the best tool for this.) In a small saucepan, add flour to the oil or melted bacon fat and whisk together. If too thick, add a bit more oil or fat. Cook on medium high heat until the mixture turns a dark brown - stir often. Now slowly pour in the milk while constantly whisking until smooth. Add 1/4 teaspoon salt and 1/2 teaspoon or more of pepper. Simmer on low heat and stir often. It will continue to thicken and you may need to add more milk. When you serve it, as it cools, it will thicken even more so you do not want it too thick when you serve it.

SAUSAGE CREAM GRAVY

Same as above, but instead of bacon fat you will fry up 1/3 cup ground sausage meat (like *Jimmy Dean*). Remove the sausage to drain and reserve 2 tablespoons of the pork fat to which you add the flour and milk as above. Add the ground pork back to the mixture when done.

COOKING & FOOD TIPS

BAKING
Baking things like cakes and cookies and other desserts requires exact measurements. Never use a little more or less of this or that. It will effect the outcome.

BOILING VEGETABLES
Whatever grows below ground (like potatoes) is placed in water and then brought to a boil. If it grows above ground it is placed in water that is already boiling.

BROWN SUGAR
When a recipe calls for brown or dark brown sugar you must pack the sugar into the measuring spoon or cup in order to be using the correct amount.

EGGS
Always cook fried eggs and scrambled eggs on a low temperature. This keeps the whites from becoming rubbery and the eggs creamy when scrambling eggs.

Crack eggs on a flat surface not the rim of a bowl to prevent getting bits of shell in your food.

Peeling a hard-boiled egg:
After you boil an egg, run it under cold water so you can handle it. Then rap each end and just peel about a quarter-sized patch off each end. Wrap one hand around the egg with the narrowest part facing up. Place your other hand at the other end of the egg. Put your mouth on the narrow end where you have peeled the shell and blow. The egg will slide right out.

Hard-boiling an egg:
You don't need to boil it for 12 minutes. You can just bring it to a boil, cover the pot and set it aside for 12 minutes.

CHICKEN
Slicing raw chicken: If you need to cut up some raw boneless/skinless chicken breasts for a stir-fry or chicken tenders it will cut more easily if it is still about half frozen when you cut it up.

Roasted Chickens at the Supermarket: Most markets these days sell roasted chickens and the price is usually good. These are also great in a pinch if you need some chicken for a recipe that requires some cooked chicken. Buy one and just pull all the meat off the bones and freeze it in 1-1/2 cup portions.

GARLIC
Peeling:
The best way to peel garlic is to place a clove on a flat surface, place the broad side of a wide knife on the clove then whack it with the side of your fist. The skin will peel off easily.

Garlic Smell on Your Finders:
After handling garlic just rub your fingers on your stainless steel sink and that will remove the smell better than soap.

BACON FAT
Don't throw out your rendered bacon fat. Let it cool and pour it into a jar and keep it in the fridge. Each time you render some bacon add the fat to the jar. It will keep for a couple of months. Just start a new jar every couple of months. Bacon fat is good. It has many uses — like making a cream gravy or a warm bacon dressing or some country green beans.

LIMP VEGETABLES
Vegetables like carrots, celery, peppers, snow peas, broccoli, cauliflower often turn soft or rubbery when they begin to get old in the fridge. You can bring them back to life by cutting them up in large pieces and placing them in a lidded container of water. Within 24 hours they will rejuvenate and become firm and crisp. Drain the water and keep them sealed in the container.

DISH SPONGE
Microwave your dish sponge or dish rag on high for 1 minute daily. Wet it and ring it out first. This will sterilize it and reduce any odor.

PASTA

For pasta to have **maximum flavor** it is always good to add some marinara or meat sauce to the cooked pasta and cook it together a few minutes so the pasta can soak in the flavor. Just pouring a sauce over pasta leaves it pretty bland. This is true for any recipe where a pasta is involved.

Do NOT add oil to pasta water — I don't care who says you should. It coats the pasta and prevents sauces from sticking to it. Pasta will not stick to itself in the pot if you stir it for a minute after you put it in the pot and give it another stir or two during boiling.

Anytime you cook a pasta dish, save some of the boiling water. It is handy if you need to thin a sauce because it contains starch. It will help make the sauce thicker and creamier.

Cooked pasta freezes well. Just put it in a pot of boiling water to reheat or microwave it in some water.

If you are using pasta in a casserole like lasagna or stuffed shells reduce the cooking time to about one-third less than the package recommends for doneness. This makes handling the pasta much easier, prevents tearing and helps the casserole to thicken as the pasta continues to absorb liquid while baking.

STRAWBERRIES

It's hard to find small, sweet strawberries like we had years ago. The current varieties we find in stores have been put on steroids. They are huge, not sweet and often hard. This can be fixed easily. Cut the strawberries in half or quarters depending on size. Sprinkle 2 or 3 tablespoons of sugar into a quart of sliced strawberries. Add 1 teaspoon lemon juice and 2 tablespoons water. Toss to coat. Let sit overnight in the fridge.(This is called *macerating*.) This also works well with peaches that might not be quite ripe.

STORING BOXED FOODS

Once I open a box or bag of anything like flour, cereal, sugar, that doesn't have a tight re-seal lid or closure I either put the contents in a plastic container or a storage bag if the bag or box will fit. Keep cornmeal in a tight container in the fridge.

CHEESE

All cheeses have fat and salt, some more than others. There are low-fat and low-salt versions of most cheeses these days, but you will sacrifice flavor and sometimes texture. Of course, if you eat cheese in moderation that isn't a problem. But if you are curious about the healthier cheeses to eat go for: parmesan, ricotta (which is a good substitute for cream cheese on a bagel). feta (though high salt), cottage cheese, goat cheese (high salt), gouda, mozzarella, swiss, neufchatel (a naturally light cream cheese), Queso Fresco and string cheese. You may have noticed that their are no "orange" cheeses in the list.

After opening cheese, rewrap it in plastic wrap or put it in an air-tight container. Mold on hard cheeses is deemed safe if you trim it off, but toss soft cheeses that get moldy.

ALUMINUM

Aluminum is a reactive metal. Salt and acids will not only damage them, but can also alter flavors of foods mixed or stored in them. If you have aluminum mixing bowls or bakeware use them only for mixing dry ingredients or with non-acidic/salty foods.

ALUMINUM FOIL

The new non-stick foil is a great invention. Anytime you bake or broil something in the oven that might stick and burn use it to line your pan, but do not use for cookies! Use parchment paper for cookies.

LEMONS

You will get more juice out of a lemon or lime if it is warm. Put it in the microwave long enough to heat it up a bit. Rolling a lemon while pressing on it for about 15 seconds will also create more juice.

SOUPS

Hearty canned soups, the kind you do not mix with water or milk, can become a meal by serving them over rice or biscuits or noodles. A "pot roast" or "beef and vegatables" soup works well for this. You can also make a quick pot pie by pouring one in a pie pan, covering with a crust and baking at 400°F until the crust is browned.

RECIPES

A stir-fry is a quick, simple and healthy dinner. Most of the work is in the prep - cutting up all your ingredients and having them ready once you begin. It's called *mise en place*, a French phrase which means "putting in place", as in set up. You should be able to make a stir-fry in 15 minutes once all the elements are prepared in advance.

There are no amounts given here because it depends on what vegetables and meats you are going to use. This recipe describes the steps to make a stir-fry. Read the entire recipe to get an idea of what is involved and what you will need.

You can use chicken, beef, pork or shrimp or no meat at all and make it vegetarian. You can also use **leftover chicken, beef or pork** cut into strips or bite sizes.

The point of a stir-fry is to cook your ingredients quickly on a high heat for a short time and retain the crispness of the vegetables. Asian restaurants use a wok for this purpose as it is especially suited to this type of cooking, but a skillet can work as well for ordinary home use.

Time: 15 minutes **Servings:** 1 **Tools:** large skillet
Ingredients: a protein, vegetables, herbs, spices, broth, cornstarch, soy sauce, rice

CHOOSE AND PREPARE YOUR PROTEIN:

If you use leftovers to do a stir-fry you will not need to cook the meat or shrimp as in Step 1. Just have it at room temperature and sliced in thin strips. Select a serving portion of one of the proteins listed below.

Chicken: cut a boneless/skinless chicken breast half in thin strips. It's easier to cut if it is partially frozen. Place strips in a bowl and set aside to thaw completely if not thawed. Sprinkle with a little soy sauce. (You can also add a little garlic powder and ground ginger.) *You could also use frozen fried chicken nuggets to imitate asian dishes that use fried bits of chicken. Precook according to directions and add in Step 3.*

Beef: Buy some pieces of top or bottom round (also called round steak. If possible buy it *tenderized or ask the butcher to tenderize it.*) Slice in thin strips. Place strips in a bowl with a little soy sauce. (You can also add a little garlic powder and ground ginger.)

Pork: Buy some individual boneless pork loins. Slice in thin strips. Place strips in a bowl with a little soy sauce. (You can also add a little garlic powder and ground ginger.)

Shrimp: You can use any kind - frozen or fresh or even the kind that come in a ring. Buy a medium size. Thaw if frozen. **Remove tails and devein if needed** (see *Shrimp* page 107). Place in a bowl with a little soy sauce. (You can also add a little garlic powder and ground ginger.)

PREPARE THE VEGETABLES, THICKENER AND AROMATICS:

- **VEGETABLES** cut in bite sizes - about 1-1/2 to 2 cups total vegetables will make a good serving. I have listed vegetables as either "hard" or "soft." This determines the cooking time as some take a little longer to reach doneness. By adding them in order you will retain crispness. Put each group of vegetables in its own bowl or in separate piles on a large plate. **If you use snow peas, keep them separate** as they go in at the very end (Step 3).You can use only 1 vegetable, like broccoli or sliced bell peppers - stir-fry is about what you want or have on hand.

> **Vegetable Options:** Some vegetables take longer to cook than others. **"Hard" vegetables:** carrots, celery, onion, mushrooms, bok choy, broccoli. **"Soft" vegetables:** any color of bell pepper, spring onion, sliced water chestnuts (canned), sliced bamboo shoots (canned), asparagus, snow peas, peanuts, cashews...

- **THICKENER:** You will need a thickening agent that will also create a sauce — 1/2 tablespoon of **cornstarch** and 1/2 cup of low-sodium canned **chicken broth** (or **beef broth** if using beef). Stir a little broth into 1/2 tablespoon of cornstarch in a measuring cup. Once blended stir in the remaning 1/2 cup of broth. Set aside. **DO NOT** add the cornstarch to broth - liquid is always added to cornstarch. It's science. Save remaining broth to thin if needed in Step 4.

- **AROMATICS:** use all or some - minced **garlic**, minced fresh or ground **ginger, red pepper flakes** (for heat if you like it a little spicy). There are also some **Asian-style sauces** at the market like Hoison Sauce, a kind of Asian BBQ sauce, or Plum Sauce, a sweet and sour sauce. These are quite pungent so a tablespoon is plenty. If you use them, cut back on the soy sauce as these have soy sauce in them already. **If you want to make a "sweet and sour"** stir-fry add a tablespoon of white or apple cider vinegar and a tablespoon of sugar to the thickening mixture above. Instead of sugar you can use **pineapple chunks** (add in Step 3) which will give it the sweetness and which are typical in "sweet and sour" dishes.

STIR-FRY

1. *(If you are using leftover cooked meat or shrimp, skip to Step 2.)* Put a large skillet on **medium high heat**. Add a few tablespoon of oil to the pan. When the oil is hot **add your raw meat or shrimp**. Keep moving it around the pan. Cook until it is no longer raw. (Shrimp is done when it just begins to curl up.) **Remove to a clean bowl.**

2. Add a little **more oil** to the pan. Add your **hard vegetables** (celery, broccoli, carrots, onion, bok choy, mushrooms, etc.) and **stir-fry - moving them around the pan constantly** for about 4 minutes. **You should hear sizzling.** You do not want the vegetables to char so you may need to adjust your temperature. Now add your **soft vegetables** and **aromatics** to the vegetables in the pan. Add **snow peas** in Step 3). Stir-fry for another 2 minutes.

3. Now add your **cooked meat or shrimp** back to the pan and add your **snow peas** if using them. Mix everything together. **Turn heat to high. Stir the thickening agent to remix it** and **immediately** pour it over the vegetables and stir everything together well. When it begins to bubble it will thicken. **Keep stirring. If it gets too thick** add some more broth and stir. You want a thin gravy not runny like water and not thick like a paste. Once it bubbles and the consistency of the sauce is right, reduce heat to low and cover the pan and simmer for **1 minute only**. Don't overcook — you want crisp vegetables.

Uncover, mix in 1 tablespoon of soy sauce, unless you used an Asian sauce. Add more broth if it has gotten too thick and mix. Taste for salt — add soy sauce if needed. Remove from heat. Serve immediately over rice.

BEEF

All beef is graded by the USDA. **USDA Prime** is the highest grade, but only about 1 to 2.5 percent is graded prime. **USDA Choice** is next in grade and you are more likely to find this grade or the grade below it, **USDA Select**. Price of the beef obviously scales with the grading. If you are buying a steak go for Choice, if possible. It should cost only a little more than Select, but the taste will be worth it.

Marbling is a term that describes how thin strands or flecks of fat run through the lean part of the meat and is a major factor in grading. You want this marbling as the fat gives flavor and makes the cut more tender and juicy. This is especially important when buying steaks.

Freshly cut meat has a bright red appearance. Unwrapped beef at the counter may be a little darker red due faster oxidation and that is okay.

Always smell the meat. If it has a strong ammonia-like odor or smells sour take it back. Always check the expiration date or sell-by date on a package of meat. If the tray is cracked or the plastic wrap is torn leave it be. If there is a lot of liquid in the package it may have been frozen and thawed which means it will not keep as long as a fresh piece of meat.

There are many of cuts of beef. There are specific ways a cut can be or should be cooked wether in a dry heat, moist heat, stewed or braised low-and-slow. Let's take a look at the most common cuts — those you are most likely to cook...

STEAK

I start here because almost everyone loves a good steak. You will pay top dollar at fine steakhouses for a good piece of meat done to perfection. It is well-known that such places get the best grades of steak. The quality of their beef is usually higher than what you can find at the grocery store. You might find higher quality at a butcher shop, but that is no guarantee. My favorite cut is the filet mignon or beef tenderloin. I used to by it at

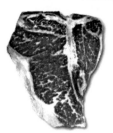

T-BONE

RIB-EYE

STRIP

FILET

a local family-owned grocery store. Their filets were killer — moist, tender, delicious beef flavor. They went out of business. I searched high and low for a filet that was equal to theirs. I tried almost every butcher shop and specialty store in my area, but to no avail. Finally I did find a filet that was its equal — at a local grocery chain. Who knew? So I guess it all depends from whom they get their beef.

Their are 4 common steak cuts: T-bone, rib-eye, strip and filet. Most people have a preference for their steak cut. The Porterhouse steak is similar to a T-bone, but the tenderloin part is larger.

COOKING A STEAK

A lot depends on the the thickness of the steak and how you like your steak done from rare to well. If you grill a thin (1/4 to 3/8 inch) rib-eye, it won't have a chance to get much grill flavor or char and if you wait for that to happen it's well done. To get grill flavor the meat has to char a bit. If you are going to grill a steak it should be at least 3/4 to 1 inch thick. If you like a rare or medium-rare steak you really can't use a steak that is less that 3/4 inch thick.

How do you know when a steak is done to your liking — rare, medium rare, medium, medium well, well-done? NEVER cut into it to check — it will start losing its juices. You can use a meat thermometer. I do it by feel. When you press on a well done steak there is very little give. If you press on a medium done steak it still has some give and softness. You can use your hand as a guide...

Open your left hand if you are right handed (if right handed do the opposite). Leave the hand somewhat relaxed. With the index finger of your right hand press on the area just below where the thumb meets the palm. It feels squishy — that's rare. Now stretch and tighten your hand and press the same area. That's medium. If you press the center of your palm that's well-done. Remember that a steak continues to cook for about 10 minutes after it is taken off the heat. The temperature will rise 5 to 10 degrees. Always err on the side of underdone because you can always throw it back on the heat for a minute or two.

And always wait 10 minutes before you cut into your steak so its juices can reabsorb into the meat.

Grilling: Generally a steak is cooked on a grill, either outdoors or indoors. Some ranges come with a grill insert. When you grill a steak you should not turn it back and forth from side to side. You cook one side, then the other.

Broiling: This is another acceptable method. Sear the first side as close to the broiler element as possible. Then flip it and sear the second side. If you want it more well done either turn down the broiler or move the pan to a lower position.

Pan-Frying: This method is probably the best for a think steak. You can get a skillet really hot and sear both sides quickly before the inside over-cooks. If you don't have a grill this method is often use to quickly sear both sides of a thick steak like a filet or rib-eye, then the steak is moved to a hot oven (450° - 500°F) to finish cooking.

CHUCK ROASTS AND SHOULDER ROASTS

These roasts used to be fairly inexpensive, but not so much anymore. All beef has gotten pricey. I always look at a price and think how many meals I will get out of it. If a roast costs $12 and I will get 4 meals out of it that's only $3 per meal and that's not bad. These roasts are usually braised or stewed for 3 to 4 hours to make them tender. They are the typical cuts used for a **pot roast** or **beef stew**.

BEEF TENDERLOIN

Beef tenderloin is a long, round cut from which we get the filet mignon. It's perhaps the most expensive cut of beef. While it may not have extensive marbling like other cuts it is tender and flavorful. It is usually grilled, broiled or roasted in the oven.

Some whole tenderloins come trimmed meaning the silver skin and a piece of meat that runs along the side of the tenderloin, the chain, have been removed. (These should also have been removed when you buy a filet mignon.) Trimmed tenderloins will be more expensive than those that are not trimmed. If you love a filet steak it is cheaper to buy a whole tenderloin, slice it in pieces and freeze them for when you want them. If you buy a whole untrimmed tenderloin ask the butcher to remove the silver skin and chain (you need skills to do that), but keep the chain. Cut the meat from the chain and use it for a stew.

One end of the loin will be smaller as it tapers to the end. It's best to cut this off before roasting because it will dry out before the rest of the loin is done. Freeze it and use it later, sliced very thin for a stir-fry or cube it and add it to a stew.

Roasting: If you roast a beef tenderloin in the oven:

1. Brush it with some oil, then salt and pepper the exterior
2. Now sear it on all sides in a hot skillet then place it on a roasting pan and move it to an oven preheated to 350°F. *(Remember - when you sear a piece of meat don't try to move it until it releases easily when you tug on it.)*
3. Roast for 30 to 45 minutes. A thermometer should read 140°F for medium - check at 30 minutes.
4. Let rest covered with foil for 10 minutes before slicing.

A light **marinade** of a few tablespoons of soy sauce, some minced garlic, a little oil, is always a nice addition to a tenderloin. Place the tenderloin in a plastic bag with the ingredients and set in the fridge for an hour or more. **Be sure to pat it dry before proceeding with the roasting recipe above.**

Grilling: Prepare as for roasting. Sear all sides on the grill, then reduce the heat as you don't want to cook it too fast or too hot.

BRISKET

Brisket is probably best known for its most common preparations as corned beef or smoked for Texas BBQ brisket, but you can roast a brisket as is and it is delicious. There is only one important thing to remember and that is it **MUST be sliced against the grain** or you cannot chew it. Briskets must be cooked  low-and-slow to become tender. (See recipe.) They will shrink by a third to a half when cooked so keep that in mind when you buy one.

FLANK STEAK, SKIRT STEAK & FLAT IRON STEAK

These cuts are similar, normally long, flat and about 3/4 to 1 inch thick. They are never cooked to well-done as they tend to get tough and dry.

FLANK STEAK   FLAT IRON STEAK

Like brisket they **must be cut against the grain** when slicing. They are often marinated to help tenderize them and give them more flavor. (The skirt steak has a thin membrane on the underside which should be pulled off before cooking.) These cuts work best grilled on high heat or seared in a skillet on high heat. The point is to sear the exterior as fast as possible before the interior gets overdone. If you marinate them, dry them before brushing with oil and sprinkling with salt and pepper. Skirt steak is typically used for fajitas.

ROUND STEAK

Round steak is a fairly versatile cut and generally needs to be cooked low-and-slow either by braising or stewing. You may find it packaged whole or cut and packaged separately in it's 3 main parts: top round, bottom round or eye of round. Sliced in thin strips it works well for a stir-fry. If you can, buy round steak that has been run through a tenderizer at the market (or ask the butcher to do it) or use a meat mallet to tenderize it.

Cube Steaks are often pieces of top round that have been pounded with a meat tenderizer (the spiky points on the mallet) so they can be pan fried quickly and still be tender.

BEEF ROASTS

You will find several types of beef roasts at the market like: **standing prime rib, rib eye, top round, bottom round** and **eye of round.** All of these are typically roasted in an oven. The standing rib roast or prime rib has a rack of bones. It is the most expensive and tastiest roast cut with a rib eye roast coming in second. The only way to truly know when one is done is to use a meat thermometer so it is cooked to your liking.

HAMBURGER

The main thing to know about hamburger are the types and their meat to fat ratio:

ground beef (70-30),
lean ground beef (no more than 22% fat),
extra-lean ground beef (no more than 15% fat),
ground round (85-15),
ground chuck (80-20) and
ground sirloin (90-10).
The higher the fat the more flavor (and less expensive) and the more shrinkage when cooked. If you use ground sirloin for a burger don't cook it well-done or it can be very dry. **Ground chuck** is typically used for hamburgers.

Chuck roasts and shoulder roasts are the typical cut of meat used for things like beef stew or what is called "pot roast." They are a very flavorful cut, but not so tender unless you cook it low and slow. You will easily get 3 to 4 meals from a roast. You can use leftovers to make a quick beef stroganoff, enchiladas, beef BBQ, beef pot pie or a vegetable beef soup. While you're at it, why not cook 2 roasts and load the freezer with portions?

Time: 15 minutes prep / 3 hour cooking
Servings: 4 to 6
Tools: Dutch Oven or roasting pan and wide aluminum foil

INGREDIENTS:

1 **chuck or shoulder roast**

1 large **onion** peeled and quartered or 1 package of *Lipton* **onion soup mix** or beefy onion soup mix or brand equivalent

3 ribs of **celery** cut in half

1 can **or** 1 bottle of **beer or** 1 can of low-sodium beef broth **or** 1/2 can beef broth and 1/2 cup red wine.

(optional) 1 tablespoon **tomato paste**

1 tablespoon of **pepper**

You may add the following if you want to cook some carrots and potatoes with the roast. Use enough carrots and potatoes for a serving you will eat or double the amount if you plan to eat leftovers and not freeze the meat for another time.

carrots sliced in 3 inches pieces

red **new potatoes left whole** or large red, white or Yukon Gold potatoes peeled and quartered

DIRECTIONS:

If you use an onion soup mix there is no need to salt the meat.

1. *Select a method for cooking:*

   Dutch Oven: If the pot is not large enough you may have to cut the roast in pieces to create a single layer. Proceed as directed for using a roasting pan. Typically the roast is browned in the Dutch Oven on the stove in a bit of oil on both sides before cooking. After searing add the liquids, soup mix or onion, celery and pepper. The Dutch Oven is covered and placed in a 300° F oven for 3 hours. Potatoes and carrots may be added in the last hour.

   Roasting Pan: Sprinkle both sides of the roast with pepper (and salt if not using an onion soup mix) and place in the pan. Sprinkle the onion soup mix into the pan on and around the meat. Add the celery (and onion if not using a mix) and liquids. Seal the pan tightly with foil. Bake at 300°F. for 3 hours. Potatoes and carrots may be added in the last hour.

2. When finished cooking remove and discard the celery and onion. Place meat and vegetables on platter and cover with foil to keep warm.

Make a gravy: You can just use the meat juices as a gravy without thickening them, but you should de-fat the juices first — pour the juices in a large measuring cup and when the fat and broth have separated use a spoon to remove most of the fat or use a gravy separator. If you want a thicker and tastier gravy, see *Gravies* page 28. You can either make a simple gravy or a gravy using the meat fat.

BEEF STROGANOFF

Typically you will either buy a package of "stew beef" (cut-up chuck roast) or a whole chuck roast that you will cut up in cubes yourself - which is the best alternative as stew beef is often tough. If you use uncooked meat it will take longer as you will need to braise the meat to make it tender. If you have leftover cooked chuck roast or round steak this makes for a quick recipe. Recipes for each method are below. **Mushrooms are key** to the flavor of this dish, so you need to use **fresh ones, not canned.**

Time: 3 hours with uncooked meat, 30 minutes with leftover beef — round steak or chuck/shoulder roast.
Servings: 2 servings with uncooked beef, 1 serving with leftover beef
Tools: large skillet with a lid (or large pot if cooking beef first)

INGREDIENTS:

Using Uncooked Beef recipe:

1 package of stew beef or 2 cups of a chuck roast cut up into 1 inch pieces. *NOTE: you can cook the entire roast cut into pieces and freeze the rest for other recipes.*

1/2 cup **flour** seasoned with 1 teaspoon each salt and pepper

4 tablespoons **oil**

2 (10 3/4-ounce) cans low-sodium **beef broth**

2 tablespoons **butter**

1/2 cup **onion**, finely chopped

8 ounces **fresh mushrooms** - crimini or portabellas - sliced

1 (10 3/4-ounce) can **cream of mushroom soup**

Salt and black pepper

1/2 cup **sour cream**

2 servings of **cooked egg noodles** *(refrigerate or freeze half of cooked noodles with the leftover stroganoff mixture for another meal)*

DIRECTIONS:

If Using Uncooked Beef:

Dredge meat pieces in flour seasoned with salt and pepper. Fry dredged meat in skillet on medium-high in the oil until browned. Add beef broth, cover and simmer for 1-1/2 hours or until meat is fork tender. Remove meat and liquid to a bowl.

1. Add 2 tablespoons butter to the skillet. Sauté onions and mushrooms until mushrooms are golden brown.

2. Add meat and broth back to the pan. Stir in mushroom soup and mix well. Simmer covered for 15 minutes.

3. Stir in sour cream and simmer uncovered for 3 minutes. If too thick add some milk.

Serve over cooked egg noodles.

If Using Leftover Beef:

Half all of the ingredients in the recipe except the mushroom soup. You will not dredge the meat in flour. A cup of cooked meat, either leftover pot roast or round steak, will be enough for a serving.

Start with Step 1 above. When mushroom are done add meat, broth and mushroom soup to the pan and mix well. Cook for 5 minutes then add sour cream and simmer 5 more minutes.

A brisket is a very flavorful cut of meat that has **one major requirement** - when you slice it you **MUST** cut it across the grain or it will be tough! Brisket must be cooked low and slow to become tender. Leftover sliced brisket makes a **great cold roast beef sandwich.** You can slice and serve the brisket when it is done baking, but it is **easier to slice** if you actually cook it early in the day or a day before and refrigerate it then slice it and reheat a portion in some beef broth. **Leftovers** can be easily reheated in a pot with some beef broth or a powdered gravy mix or a quick gravy.

Time: 4 hours
Servings: depends on size of brisket
Tools: large shallow roasting pan (like a broiler pan), wide aluminum foil

INGREDIENTS:

1 **beef brisket** (They come in all sizes. The measurements below are for a medium sized brisket - 3-4 pounds)

I am including 3 options for flavoring the brisket...

Option 1:

2 medium (size of a baseball) or 1 large **onion** cut in 1/4 inch slices

salt and pepper

Option 2:

2 medium (size of a baseball) or 1 large **onion** cut in 1/4 inch slices

4 tablespoon **chili sauce** (*Bennet's* is preferred. Other brands are not nearly as good.)

salt and pepper

Option 3:

1 package of *Lipton's* Onion Soup mix or equivalent brand

NO SALT

pepper

DIRECTIONS:

1. Pat brisket dry. There may be some large pieces of fat on the brisket. You do not want to remove all of it, but you may remove some of the excess. Salt and pepper both sides of the brisket. Use lots of pepper.

2. Place a large piece of foil - about 6 inches wider and longer than the meat - in the shallow roasting pan. Put half of your seasoning options (onions, chili sauce, soup mix) on the foil where you will place the brisket. Place the brisket on top, fat side up.

3. Spread the remainder of your desired seasonings on the fatty side of the brisket.

4. Tear off a piece of foil the same size as the bottom. Place it on top and seal all 4 edges.

5. Bake at 300°F for 4 hours.

6. Remove the brisket. Open one end of the aluminum bag, bend the foil into a spout and pour off the liquid into a glass measuring cup or gravy separator. Close the foil and let the brisket rest for about 20 minutes in the foil.

7. Remove the brisket. Scrape off any coating so you can see the grain of the meat. You might want to cut it into 2 or 4 pieces to make slicing easier. Slice it thinly **AGAINST THE GRAIN** of the meat, *not with the grain.* (Think of it like a piece of wood.) The juices will have separated in the measuring cup. Remove the fat. You can use the liquid to moisten the meat. A little heated beef broth will work as well. Don't use the fat to make a gravy — brisket fat is not a good flavor.

BARBECUE

A recipe for a hamburger, beef or pork barbecue for sandwiches. If you have 1 cup of leftover pork, any kind, or leftover beef from a pot roast you can use it to make a pork or beef barbecue. Leftover beef brisket makes a delicious beef barbecue as well.

Time: 1 hour
Servings: 3 to 4
Tools: medium saucepan with a lid

HAMBURGER BBQ

INGREDIENTS:	DIRECTIONS:
1 pound **ground chuck**	1. Brown the ground beef in a medium saucepan on medium high heat. Drain of grease and return to pot.
1 medium **onion** chopped	
1/2 cup chopped **green bell pepper**	
3/4 cup **ketchup**	2. Add onion to ground beef and continue to cook until onions are soft - 7 minutes.
1 tablespoon **cider vinegar**	
1 small can (8 oz.) **tomato sauce**	3. Add rest of ingredients and simmer uncovered for at least 30 minutes - longer for more flavor. You want the water to cook out so it becomes thick.
1/2 cup **water**	
1 teaspoon **Worcestershire sauce**	
2 tablespoons **brown sugar**	
1 teaspoon **dry ground mustard**	
2 teaspoons each of **salt and pepper**	

PORK OR BEEF BBQ

These directions are for **1 cup of leftover beef or pork** that has been shredded or chopped somewhat small.

Add about 1/3 cup of chopped onion to a small saucepan with a little oil. Sauté until soft - about 5 minutes. Add your leftover pork or beef to the onion and add:
1/2 cup **ketchup**
1/3 cup chopped **green bell pepper**
1/2 cup **water**
1 tablespoon **cider vinegar**
1 teaspoon **Worcestershire sauce**
1 tablespoon **brown sugar**
1 teaspoon **dry ground mustard**
2 teaspoons each of **salt and pepper**
1 teaspoon **cumin or chili powder**

Simmer for 30 minutes or until thick.

Meatloaf is a standard American comfort food. You can use all ground beef, but a mixture of beef and ground pork makes a better taste and has less fat or use ground turkey and ground pork for an even leaner meatloaf. Ground meat usually comes in 1 pound packages. If you use a mix of beef and pork you can double the amounts in this recipe to make a large meatloaf *or* save 1/2 pound of each to use later for another meatloaf or make meatballs or a meat marinara.

Leftovers can be frozen and either heated in the oven (300°F.) in some foil or "fried" in a skillet on medium-low heat. You can also chop it up and add it to a marinara to make a meat sauce.

Time: 15 minutes prep / 45 minutes to 1 hour cooking time
Servings: 3-4
Tools: meatloaf pan, small roasting pan or dish, or a pie pan or a bread pan

INGREDIENTS:

1 pound **ground chuck** or a mix of 1/2 pound ground chuck and 1/2 pound **ground pork** for leaner meatloaf.

1/3 cup each of **carrot, celery and onion - chopped very fine** or pulverized in a food processor/blender (*If you double the recipe use 1/2 cup each.*)

(optional) add 1/4 cup **green bell pepper** to the above

1 **egg**

2 teaspoon **salt**

1 teaspoon black **pepper**

1 teaspoon worcestershire sauce

2 tablespoons **ketchup**

1/2 tablespoon **dijon or brown mustard**

1/2 cup **breadcrumbs mixed into 1/4 cup milk**

DIRECTIONS:

1. Mix well all the ingredients in a large mixing bowl. It's easiest to just use some clean hands to mush it all together. Now form it into a loaf or a round - whichever you prefer. Select a baking dish appropriate to the form. You do not want the loaf to touch the sides of the dish. If it does the loaf will cook in its own fat and that's not good. Some people put slices of white bread under the loaf to soak up the fat and prevent the loaf from absorbing the fat that is released while cooking.

2. Top meatloaf with some additional ketchup.

3. Bake at 400°F for 45 minutes to 1 hour. Let rest for 10 minutes before slicing. **If you double the recipe** it will need to cook for 60 to 75 minutes. (Internal temperature of 160°F.)

ROAST BEEF

A beef roast is a major comfort food and very simple to make. I am including 2 recipes. You need a deep roasting pan with a rack insert for the first one or a Dutch oven for the second one.

Time: 2-1/2 hours
Servings: several
Tools: roasting pan with rack or Dutch oven

INGREDIENTS:

1 **beef top round**, 4-5 pounds

kosher salt

fresh ground black **pepper**

1/4 cup **Dijon mustard**

juice of 1/2 **lemon**

(optional) washed and dried new **potatoes** (enough for how many servings you need — figure 4 or 5 per person)

DIRECTIONS: ROASTING PAN

Preheat oven to 500°F.

1. Season all sides of the roast with salt and pepper. Combine mustard and lemon juice and rub it all over the beef.

2. Place the beef on the rack in the roasting pan. Place the potatoes under the rack beneath the beef roast. Sprinkle them with salt and pepper.

3. Place in the center of the oven. After 10 minutes reduce the heat to 350°F. Figure 10 minutes a pound for medium rare (internal temperature of 130°F). Medium — 150°F. Cover and let rest for 15 minutes before slicing. Pour pan juices over potatoes to serve.

INGREDIENTS:

1 **beef top round**, 4-5 pounds

2 teaspoons **salt**

1 tablespoon black **pepper**

1 **onion** sliced in 1/4 inch rings

1 rib **celery** cut in 3 pieces

1 **carrot** peeled and cut in large pieces

3 cans **low-sodium beef broth**

Thickening Slurry: add 1/4 cup **water** to 2 tablespoons **cornstarch** and mix until smooth.

DIRECTIONS: DUTCH OVEN

Preheat oven to 275°F.

1. Season all sides of the roast with salt and pepper.

2. Heat 3 tablespoons of oil in a Dutch oven and brown meat on all sides on medium high heat. Remove beef from pot and set aside.

3. Add onions, celery and carrot to pot and set beef, fat side up, on top of the onions. Pour in beef broth.

4. Cook in oven, uncovered. Figure 10 minutes a pound for medium rare (internal temperature of 130°F). Medium — 150°F. When done, remove to platter, cover and let rest for 15 minutes before slicing. Remove vegetables from pot. Make a slurry with cornstarch and water, add to pot, bring to boil while constantly stirring to thicken. Add water if too thick.

SWISS STEAK

Swiss steak uses the beef cut called Round Steak — a very versatile cut of beef. It is one of the leanest cuts which means it can also be the toughest, but by braising it (cooking it low and slow in a liquid) it can become tender.

Time: 3 hours
Servings: 3 to 4
Tools: large mixing bowl and 9" x 13" baking dish or deep roasting pan or Dutch Oven
Serve with: mashed potatoes, green vegetable

INGREDIENTS:

1 **Round Steak** cut into serving size pieces **or 8 pieces** of pre-cut bottom round. <u>If you can, buy round steak that has been run through a tenderizer at the market or use the meat mallet to tenderize it.</u>

1, 32 ounce can of **diced tomatoes**

2 tablespoons of **tomato paste**

1 can low-sodium beef broth

1 cup **water**

1 large **onion** chopped

1 large **green pepper** chopped

salt and pepper

1 teaspoon **paprika**

DIRECTIONS:

1. Dredge the meat pieces in flour, shake off excess flour, then pound pieces with tenderizer mallet.

2. Heat a large skillet to medium-high, add a few table-spoons of oil and sear 3 or 4 pieces of the meat on both sides for about 2 -3 minutes. You will have to do this in batches removing the cooked pieces to a 9" x 13" baking dish or a deep roasting pan or a Dutch Oven.

3. When all the meat is done, mix the diced tomatoes, tomato paste, onions, broth, salt and pepper, paprika in a large bowl.

4. Pour the mixture over the meat in the 9" x 13" baking dish or roasting pan). Cover with foil or lid. Place in a 350°F oven. Bake for 2 hours covered. Remove cover, add green pepper and push them into the liquid and bake another hour uncovered.

If the finished dish seems a little thin or watery you can thicken it a bit with a cornstarch slurry...

Stir 1/4 cup of water into 2 tablespoons of cornstarch. (**ALWAYS** add liquid **TO** cornstarch, not visa-versa!) Mix to create a slurry. Remove the meat to a plate and pour the liquids into a medium saucepan. Stir half of the slurry into the liquid in the pot. Bring liquid to a simmer a cook for 1 minute. It should begin to thicken. If you like it thicker add the rest of the slurry while stirring the liquid and simmer for 2 minutes.

CHICKEN

Americans eat more chicken than any other food product. And there is a good reason — it is so versatile. There are so many ways to prepare it. Hence, you will find many chicken recipes here.

Most people have their favorite part of the chicken. White meat (the breast) has less flavor and can be dry. Dark meat (thigh and leg) has more flavor and tends to stay more moist. Wings, a mix of white and dark meat, have little meat, but because their is so much bone, they have lots of flavor and tend to have sweet meat. I used to eat nothing but the breasts, but now I find I am eating more thighs because they have more flavor and are more moist. And now you can find boneless/skinless thighs at the market and use them in place of chicken breast cutlets in recipes that use them. A package of breasts with bone and skin will usually say: "split" chicken breasts which means the whole breast that spans both sides of the chicken and divided by the breast bone has been split in half yielding 2 pieces of breast.

In the market you find an array of packaged chicken. You can buy whole roasters, a whole chicken cut up or packages of just breasts, thighs, legs or wings. You will find bone-in with skin on and boneless, skinless breasts and thighs. You will find chicken tenders — a piece of tender breast rib meat. You can find breasts that have been sliced thinly to use when you need a cutlet - these do not have to be pounded thin like a regular breast. In the freezer section you will find bags of frozen chicken breasts that have been pounded into cutlets. These are great if you do not want to pound a boneless/skinless breast. You will find all types of chicken like nuggets and tenders that are pre-breaded and that just need to be baked in an oven. Most of the nuggets are not actual pieces of chicken, but a ground chicken product formed into bite-size shapes, coated and pre-cooked.

Cross-contamination:
A big concern with chicken is bacteria that can cause serious illness. So chicken should always be well-refrigerated or frozen and thawed properly. (See Thawing Meats in the Appendix.) After you touch raw chicken you should always wash your hands with soap and any utensils and cutting boards or surfaces that come in contact with raw chicken must be cleaned well. Cutting boards are dangerous because they have miniscule cuts that you cannot see with the naked eye. These cuts are a good breeding ground for bacteria. Many people have a separate cutting board just for chicken so if there is ever any contamination it is not spread by cross-contamination when other meats or vegetables are cut on the same board.

When you open a package of chicken it should have no smell. If you can smell it — don't eat it.

Chicken is done when it is no longer pink and/or it's juices run clear, not pink.

Prepping a Chicken:
If you are going to roast a whole chicken or bake, stew or fry chicken pieces you should rinse it inside and out under cold running water then place it on some paper towel to drain and pat dry.

When you buy a whole roaster chicken wrapped in plastic you always need to check the cavity. The neck, heart, gizzard, liver are often placed in there, maybe in a bag. Be sure to remove it! If you are going to stew a whole chicken toss them in the pot to add more flavor to the broth or freeze them for a time when you are going to do so.

Bone-in/Skin on: Chicken that has a bone and skin has more flavor. If you are going to stew chicken or boil it or cook it in a recipe like Chicken Cacciatore you want to buy it this way.

Boneless/Skinless: Chicken without skin and bones is ideal for recipes that use a cutlet - a flattened piece of chicken that is pan-fried or coated and baked in the oven.

Marinades: Chicken takes well to marinades and when baking or pan-frying a simple bone-less/skinless breast it's a good way to give a bland piece of chicken more flavor.

STEWING

Some recipes call for chicken to be pre-cooked like Chicken and Dumplings. Others need shredded or chopped pieces of cooked chicken. Stewing (boiling, poaching) is an easy method to do this. You can also roast it. The advantage of stewing is the broth you will create that can be used for other recipes or the recipe itself. Homemade broth is so much better than canned.

You always use chicken with bone and skin because that is where the broth gets it flavor. I like to cook at least twice as much chicken as I need and freeze the leftovers for other meals. It just makes sense to stew more than you need. I usually stew either breasts or thighs — 1 breast or 2 thighs as a serving.

Put the cleaned chicken in a large pot. Cover with water. Add a few ribs of **celery** cut in large pieces, a few **carrots** peeled and cut in half and a small **onion** peeled and cut in half. Tuck the vegetables down into the water around the chicken. Season the water with a few teaspoons of **salt and pepper**. Bring to a boil, cover and reduce to a simmer. Cook for at least an hour. The longer you cook it the more tender it becomes.

When done, remove the chicken to a plate to cool. Once the chicken has cooled for about 15 minutes you can remove the skin and pick the meat off the bones or not. Set aside any you need for a recipe you are going to prepare now. Freeze the leftovers in serving sizes in covered containers covered with some of the broth.

Strain the broth into a large gravy separator or measuring cup. Wait about 15 minutes for the fat and broth to separate. Skim off the fat. If you are going to make a scratch chicken gravy, save the fat or freeze it for another time when you want to make a chicken gravy. If you used a gravy separator just pour the broth into another container. Freeze any broth you do not need for a recipe you are making now or pour it over saved portions of chicken you are going to freeze or just freeze it in containers for another use.

You can use frozen and thawed portions to make chicken salad or chicken enchiladas or Chicken and Dumplings or a Chicken Pot Pie.

PAN FRYING

A recipe like Chicken Cacciatore (see recipe) benefits from pan-frying the **chicken with bone and skin** first. You will clean and pat the chicken pieces dry. You heat a little oil in a large skillet on medium high heat that has a lid. You dredge the chicken pieces in flour, shake off the excess flour and place in the skillet skin side down. When the skin side is golden brown you turn the chicken and brown the second side. The chicken will not be cooked through at this point. It's at this point the chicken is removed from the pan and one of two things happen:

1. Some kind of liquid and vegetables and seasonings are added to the skillet and prepared for a short time. Then the chicken is placed back in the skillet skin side up. The skillet is covered and the contents are simmered for at least 40 minutes.

2. The chicken is placed on a roasting pan and baked at 400°F. for 40 minutes.

Other recipes, like Chicken Marsala, use boneless/skinless breast or thighs pounded thinly and then browned in the skillet. These cutlets cook quickly.

If you don't want to make a fancy recipe with a cutlet, just pound the boneless/skinless breast or thigh thinly, marinate it for 30 minutes, dry off the marinade, dredge it in flour and lightly fry it in a medium high heat skillet for about 3 to 5 minutes per side. **You don't have to pound the chicken, but** it will take more time to cook and a marinade will take longer to infuse the chicken. If you are not going to pound the chicken I highly recommend you at least butterfly a breast so it cooks faster and more evenly. If you do not know how to do this I suggest you "google" *butterfly a chicken breast* and watch a video on the technique.

If you don't want to marinate the chicken cutlet, just dredge it in some flour, shake off excess and fry it on medium high heat until golden brown on both sides and cooked through. Drizzle some lemon over it or cover it with some warmed salsa or some chopped bell peppers that have been sautéed.

CHICKEN AND DUMPLINGS

This is one of my favorite "go-to" quick and easy recipes and it is always satisfying. The dumplings are not the traditional flat kind. These are light and airy and much less work and way better than using biscuits.

Time: 60 minutes / 30 with leftovers   **Servings:** 1
Tools: medium deep pot with lid
Serve with: a salad or green vegetable

TIP: Always use chicken with skin and bones for this recipe. Chicken breasts usually come 2 in a package and thighs 4 in a package. Cook all the chicken and feeze half with half of the broth to make this dish again. Remove skin before freezing. To make this dish with the frozen chicken thaw it, place it in the pot with the broth and begin with Step 3. If you just have 1 breast or 2 thighs (a portion) use half of the recipe amounts below.

INGREDIENTS:

2 **chicken breasts or 4 thighs:**

2, 14 ounce cans **low-sodium chicken broth**

1 cup **water**

2 ribs of **celery** cut in 3 pieces

half of a small **onion**

2 **carrots** cut in 3 pieces

1 teaspoon **salt** and **pepper**

1 cup **baking mix** (like *Bisquik* or a non-name brand equivalent)

1/3 cup **milk**

pepper

(optional) 1 tablespoon chopped **parsley**

TIP: you can add peas and sliced carrots in Step 2 to have a complete meal with vegetables.

DIRECTIONS:

1. Place raw chicken in the pot, add broth, water, celery, onion, carrot. Cover, bring to a boil, reduce to a simmer and cook for 30 minutes. When the chicken is done turn off the heat. Remove the chicken to a plate and remove the skin. Remove the celery, carrot and onion from the broth and discard. Pour the broth into a gravy separator.

2. After 5 minutes pour 2 cups of the broth back into the pot. Place 1 breast or 2 thighs in the broth. Freeze remaining chicken.

NOTE: If using previously stewed and frozen chicken with broth you may omit the celery, onion and carrot. Just place the thawed chicken and 2 cups of chicken broth in a pot and bring it to a boil.

3. In a small bowl mix together the baking mix, milk and 1 teaspoon pepper (and parsley). It will be a thick sticky dumpling mixture.

4. Bring the broth with the chicken to a low boil. Now drop heaping tablespoon of the dumpling mixture on top of the broth around the pot. You will get 5 or 6 dumplings. Cook uncovered for exactly 10 minutes. The dumplings will expand.

5. After 10 minutes cover the pot and reduce heat to a level that keeps it at a light boil. Cook another 10 minutes.

A robust, classic italian chicken dish made with tomatoes, onion, bell peppers and mushrooms.

Time: 1 hour
Servings: 2
Tools: large, deep skillet with a lid or Dutch Oven
Serve with: a salad, crusty bread

INGREDIENTS:

4 **chicken thighs or** 2 **chicken breasts** halves with skin and bone-in

1/2 cup all purpose **flour**, for dredging **seasoned** with 1 teaspoons **salt** and black **pepper**

3 tablespoons **olive oil**

1/2 cup **red** or **yellow** or **green** bell pepper, chopped in 1/2 inch squares

1/2 cup **onion**, chopped in 1/2 inch squares

3 **garlic** cloves, finely chopped

1 (28-ounce) can **diced tomatoes with juice**

1/4 cup **dry white wine** (or substitute chicken broth)

3/4 cup reduced-sodium **chicken broth**

1 1/2 teaspoons dried **oregano**

1 teaspoon of dried **basil**

(optional) 2 tablespoons drained **capers**

(optional) 4 ounces of **fresh sliced mushrooms** or a small can of sliced mushrooms

DIRECTIONS:

1. Rinse chicken pieces under cold water, pat dry and place on a plate. On another plate or in a bowl, mix flour, salt and pepper. Dredge the chicken pieces in the flour to lightly coat and return to plate..

2. In a heavy, large, deep skillet or Dutch Oven, heat the olive oil over medium heat. When the oil is hot, cook the chicken until browned on both sides. Remove pieces from the pan and set aside.

3. In the same pan over medium heat, add the onion, bell pepper, mushrooms and garlic and cook for about 5 minutes - until onion is tender and mushrooms are browned.

4. Add the tomatoes with their juice, the broth, wine, capers, basil and oregano. Return the chicken pieces to the pan skin side up. Bring the sauce to a simmer. Cover and cook for 30 minutes, then uncover and simmer for 10 to 15 minutes more to reduce the liquid.

5. Spoon off any excess fat from atop the sauce.

6. Serve with spaghetti or egg noodles.

This is a simplified Cordon Bleu recipe, hence the "Bleu-ish." In the classic dish a thin chicken cutlet is filled with ham and cheese and rolled up, but in this recipe it will be open-faced which means it requires less cooking skill.

Time: 30 minutes
Servings: 1
Tools: medium (non-stick preferred) skillet,
small (non-stick preferred) roasting pan or baking sheet
Serve with: a salad or green vegetable or some egg noodles with butter and parsley

INGREDIENTS:

1 chicken cutlet (a boneless, skinless chicken breast pounded to 1/4 inch thick. You can also find think-cut breasts packaged at the market if you don't want to pound your own, but they will not be quite as tender.)

1/4 cup **breadcrumbs** or corn flake crumbs

a few **thin slices of ham** (you can use some leftover ham or some deli slices)

1/2 cup shredded or thinly sliced **swiss cheese**

salt and **pepper**

DIRECTIONS:

1. **Prepare your cutlet** - pat a boneless/skinless breast dry and place it between 2 pieces of plastic wrap about 12 inches square. On a stable, flat surface, using a meat mallet, pound the breast from the center out until you reach the desired thickness.

2. Coat one side with crumbs by pressing them into the meat. Add a little salt and pepper. Then do the same with the other side. Let it sit on a plate for 5 minutes so the crumbs adhere well.

3. In a medium-high non-stick skillet with a few tablespoons of oil, sauté the cutlet on both sides until brown - about 3 - 4 minutes per side. You don't want it to brown before the center is done so watch your heat level and adjust accordingly.

4. Place the cutlet on a piece of foil on a small roasting pan (if you have a non-stick pan no need for the foil), place the slices of ham on top and then top with the swiss cheese.

5. Place the pan in the oven on a middle rack, and set your broiler to high. When the cheese melts and begins to bubble and begins to brown it's done. Don't let the cheese burn. You will need to check its progress often (every 2 minutes) as things change under a broiler quickly!

CLASSIC VERSION:

After you pound the cutlet, place the ham and some thin slices of swiss cheese on the cutlet. Roll it up and secure it will toothpicks. Pat it with the crumbs and sprinkle with salt and pepper. Brown the roll on all sides in an oiled skillet then place it on a greased roasting pan in a 350°F oven and bake 30-35 minutes or until chicken is no longer pink. Remove toothpicks and serve.

This might be one of my favorite fast chicken dishes. How can it not be with mushrooms and cream, though you can use milk to make it lighter in fats. This French recipe (*Supremes de Volaille aux Champignons*) was popularized by Julia Child.

Time: 30 minutes
Servings: 1
Tools: medium skillet
Serve with: rice or egg noodles and a salad or vegetable

INGREDIENTS:

1 chicken breast cutlet or 2 thigh cutlets pounded to 1/4 inch thick

1/3 cup sliced **crimini mushrooms**

1 minced **shallot** or 1 tablespoon minced onion

1/4 cup **dry vermouth or dry white wine**

1/4 cup **chicken stock**

1/2 cup (4 ounces) **heavy cream or half-and-half or milk**

1 tablespoon **oil**

2 tablespoons **butter**.

1/2 tablespoon chopped fresh **parsley**

DIRECTIONS:

1. Clean the mushrooms and remove stems (if whole) and slice thinly. Set aside. Mince the shallot or onion and set aside.

2. Preheat a stainless steel skillet over medium-high heat. Pat the cutlet dry and season both sides with salt and pepper.

3. When the skillet is hot add 1 tablespoon oil and 2 tablespoons butter.

4. Place the chicken in the skillet and cook until golden brown, then flip and brown the other side, about 3 to 4 minutes per side. Remove to a plate.

5. If their is no oil or butter left in the skillet add 1 tablespoon of butter. Add shallots and mushrooms to the pan and sauté on medium heat until the mushrooms have released all their water and are golden brown, about 5 to 7 minutes.

6. Turn the heat to medium-high, add vermouth to deglaze the pan. Scrape the bottom of the pan to release any browned bits. Now add the chicken stock and boil until the liquid is reduced to 1/3.

7. Add any juices that have come off the chicken on the plate and the cream to the pan and stir. Place the chicken back in the pan. Simmer until the cream sauce thickens and coats the back of a spoon.

8. Pour sauce over chicken on your plate and garnish with fresh chopped parsley.

> *I cook with wine, sometimes I even add it to the food.*
> W.C. FIELDS

A simple, quick, classic dish with a mushroom and wine sauce.

Time: 20 minutes
Servings: 1
Tools: large skillet
Serve with: mashed potatoes or rice and green vegetable

INGREDIENTS:

2 boneless/skinless **chicken thighs or** 1 boneless/skinless **chicken breast** pounded to 1/4 inch thick.

4 ounces **crimini** (baby portabellas) **or porcini mushrooms** - stems removed and sliced thinly

3 tablespoons **olive oil**

1/4 cup **Marsala wine** (*found at the market near the oils and vinegars*)

1/4 cup **chicken broth**

1 tablespoon **butter**

1/2 tablespoon fresh chopped **parsley**

flour (for breading - about 1/2 cup mixed with 1 teaspoon salt and pepper) on a dinner size plate.

DIRECTIONS:

1. Heat the oil over medium-high flame in a large skillet.

2. When the oil is nice and hot, dredge (coat) both sides of the chicken cutlets in the seasoned flour, shaking off the excess.

3. Slip the cutlet(s) into the pan, reduce heat to medium, and fry for 4-5 minutes on each side until golden, turning once.

4. Remove the chicken to a clean plate.

5. Add the mushrooms and sauté until they are nicely browned and their moisture has evaporated, about 5-7 minutes; season with salt and pepper.

6. Pour the Marsala in the pan and boil down for a few seconds to cook out the alcohol. Add the chicken broth and simmer for a minute to reduce the sauce slightly. Stir in the butter and return the chicken to the pan; simmer gently for 1-2 minutes to heat the chicken through. Garnish with chopped parsley before serving.

CHICKEN PICCATA

This is a fast, simple, tasty, light and fresh way to prepare chicken.

Time: 30 minutes
Serving: 1
Tools: frying pan.
Serve with: mashed potatoes or rice and green vegetable

INGREDIENTS:

1 boneless/skinless **chicken** breast half, pounded to 1/4 inch thickness

1/4 cup **dry white wine**

1/2 teaspoon minced **garlic**

1/4 cup **chicken broth**

1 tablespoon fresh **lemon juice**

1 tablespoon **capers**, drained

2 tablespoon **butter**

fresh **lemon slices (optional)**

1 tablespoon chopped fresh **parsley**

seasoned flour for dredging cutlet

DIRECTIONS:

1. Dredge cutlet in seasoned (salt and pepper) flour and shake off excess.

2. Sauté cutlet in a pan with a few tablespoons of olive oil on medium heat until golden brown on each side. Remove to a plate and place in a warm oven. Should only take a few minutes each side if they are thin.

3. Add 1 tablespoon butter and 1/2 tablespoon of flour to wet pan and stir in. Cook for 1 minute.

4. Add white wine to deglaze the pan while stirring to incorporate the roux you just made. Boil to reduce to half.

5. Add chicken broth, garlic, capers and lemon juice and return cutlets to pan. Simmer for a few minutes to fully reheat cutlets. Place cutlet on a warm plate.

6. Remove pan from heat and add 1 tablespoon butter. If too thick add some chicken stock. This is a thin sauce, not a gravy. Stir to melt the butter. Pour over cutlet. Sprinkle with fresh parsley.

CHICKEN PARMESAN

You certainly can use a jar marinara sauce for this recipe, but the quick marinara below is much fresher tasting and better for you. If you choose to make the marinara, make it before you start the chicken. You can use pre-packaged chicken cutlets which are available at most supermarkets or pound out your own from a boneless/skinless chicken breast or thighs.

Oven Temp: Broiler
Time: 30 minutes
Servings: 1
Tools: frying pan and a small sheet pan, medium sauce pan
Serve with: spaghetti and a salad

INGREDIENTS:

1 boneless/skinless **chicken** breast half, pounded to 1/4 inch thickness

1/2 cup shredded **mozzarella or provolone** (or slices enough to cover the cutlet)

1/2 cup **breadcrumbs**

1/4 cup **finely grated parmesan cheese**

olive oil

Quick Marinara:

1, 14 ounce can **diced tomatoes**

1/2 of a 6 ounce can of **tomato paste** (freeze leftover paste in some plastic wrap)

1 medium **onion** diced

2 cloves **garlic** diced **or** 1 teaspoon garlic powder

2 tablespoon **olive oil**

1/2 tablespoon **oregano**

salt and pepper

DIRECTIONS:

1. Make the marinara: In a medium saucepan add olive oil, garlic and onion. Sauté for 5 minutes until onions are tender. Add diced tomatoes, tomato paste, salt and pepper and oregano. Bring to a boil then reduce heat and simmer until the sauce thickens.

2. Coat the chicken with the breadcrumbs. Let rest for 5 minutes.

3. Place the breaded cutlet in a pan heated to medium-high heat with a few tablespoons of olive oil. Fry on each side until golden – 3 to 4 minutes a side. Remove to a small baking sheet or pan.

4. Sprinkle with half of the parmesan cheese. Cover with mozzarella cheese. Then put 1/3 cup of the marinara on top of the cheese. Place on the center rack of the oven under the broiler until cheese melts and starts to bubble and brown. Remove and sprinkle with remaining parmesan cheese and fresh parsley if you have it.

If having a side of spaghetti, cook the pasta, drain and toss with some of the remaining marinara and warm through.

This is a good way to use leftover chicken or chicken you stewed and froze. A whole pie is a lot for one person, so you will have to refrigerate the leftovers and eat another day for lunch or dinner. If you want a bottom crust, too, make sure the filling has cooled before you put it in or the bottom crust will be very soggy. **BEEF POT PIE:** *substitute leftover pot roast for chicken and use low-sodium beef broth instead of chicken broth.*

Time: 1 hour to 90 minutes   **Servings:** 2 to 3
Tools: pie pan, medium saucepan
Serve with: a salad

INGREDIENTS:

1 pie crust — the kind that come 2 in a package rolled up in the dairy case.

Thaw one pie crust if it's a frozen variety. Let it sit at room temperature about 30 minutes. If it's refrigerated, let it sit out for about 20.

1-1/2 cups shredded or chopped cooked **chicken**

2 tablespoons **butter**

1/3 cup thinly **sliced carrots**

1/3 cup **chopped onion**

2 tablespoons **flour**

1/3 cup frozen **peas**

1/3 cup **cooked diced potatoes** or you can use some canned potatoes

1 cup **low-sodium chicken broth**

1/2 cup of **cream**, half-and-half or milk.

1/2 teaspoon **thyme** or poultry seasoning

(optional) 1/3 cup frozen corn

1 **egg** beaten with 1 tablespoon of water

DIRECTIONS:

If you do not have leftover chicken you will need to boil some chicken in water for about 30 minutes. One large chicken breast or 3 medium thighs should provide enough chicken. When it cools, remove bone and skin if it has any, and shred. **If not using canned potatoes**, peel a small potato, cut in 1/2 inch cubes and boil until tender.

Preheat oven to 400°F.

1. In a medium saucepan, sauté carrot and onion in 2 tablespoons of butter for about 5 minutes. Add the flour, mix and cook for 2 minutes stirring often.

2. Stir in the chicken broth, cream, thyme, 1/2 teaspoon salt and pepper and bring to a light boil. Cook for 2 minutes. If too thick, add some broth. Mix in the frozen peas and corn. (They do not have to cook.) Remove from heat. Pour into the pie pan. **Let the filling cool before adding the crust.**

3. Using a pastry brush, brush the beaten egg mixture around the rim of the pie pan. This will help the crust to adhere. Unroll the thawed (if frozen) pie crust carefully and place it on top of the pie pan. Slightly press the edges onto the rim. Fold up and over any crust hanging over the rim and press it into the crust beneath it. It doesn't have to be pretty! Use a pastry brush to coat the entire crust with the egg wash. Make 4, 1/2 slits around the crust with a sharp knife.

4. Place the pie on a rimmed baking sheet (in case of bubble-over), place in oven and bake for 35 to 45 minutes — until the crust is golden brown and you can see the mixture bubbling through the slits. Let cool 15 minutes before serving.

CHICKEN (OR TURKEY) TETRAZZINI

This is a great casserole. It is a large recipe, but serving portions can be frozen and reheated. You could buy a plain roasted chicken at the supermarket and pick off the meat for this recipe. A great way to use left-over turkey or chicken.

Time: 90 minutes
Serving: 6 - 8
Tools: 9" by 13" glass baking dish, large mixing bowl, sauté pan.
Serve with: a salad, cranberry sauce, crusty bread

INGREDIENTS:

3 cups **shredded cooked turkey or chicken** (if using chicken, thighs are best for flavor - 6 cooked thighs should do it, or 3 cooked chicken breasts)

8 ounces **sour cream**

12 ounces cooked **angel hair or vermicelli or spaghetti pasta** (break into short pieces before cooking)

1 can **cream of chicken soup** (*use Campbells - do not use low fat/"healthy" versions*)

1 can **cream of mushroom soup** (*use Campbells - do not use low fat /"healthy" versions*)

1/4 cup **parmesan cheese** (plus 1/4 cup parmesan cheese for the topping)

4 ounces **whole cream**

1-1/2 cups **frozen peas** (no need to pre-cook them, do not use canned as they will mash up)

1/4 teaspoon **nutmeg**

1/4 cup fresh chopped **parsley**

(**optional**) 1 small jar of **pimento** or 1/2 cup diced red bell pepper

8 ounces sliced crimini or portabella **mushrooms** (canned mushrooms are not a good substitute!)

2 tablespoons **butter**

1/3 cup **white wine** (or chicken broth)

DIRECTIONS:

1. Sauté mushrooms in butter in a skillet until browned and water has cooked out of the mushrooms. Deglaze the pan with the white wine (or broth) and simmer to reduce liquid in half. Then add mushrooms and remaining liquid to the mixture below.

2. Put all the remaining ingredients and cooked mushrooms/liquid in a large mixing bowl.

3. Mix everything well and pour into a greased 9" by 13" glass baking dish. Sprinkle top with 1/4 cup parmesan cheese and a little paprika.

4. Cover dish with foil and place in a 450°F oven. Check it in 15 or 20 minutes. When it is bubbling remove the foil, reduce heat to 400°F and bake for another 30 - 45 minutes. You will know it is done if you jiggle the dish and the mixture does not jiggle, but appears "set," not soupy. Remove from oven, cover with foil and let sit for at least 15 minutes for it to set before serving.

This is a great way to make "fried" chicken without all of the frying fat and standing over a bubbling pan of oil. This recipe is for a whole cut-up chicken (8 pieces), but you can adjust according to what you want to cook. Example: If you want to cook just 6 chicken wings or 4 thighs, use half the butter, but use a smaller baking dish like a pie plate or a 9" x 9" baking dish. Glass is preferred over metal.

Oven Temp: 450°F.
Time: 60 minutes
Servings: 3 to 4
Tools: 9" x 13" glass baking dish
Serve with: mashed potatoes or rice and green vegetable

INGREDIENTS:

1 **chicken** cut up (or 8 pieces)

Brining chicken keeps it moist. If you have time this is highly recommended. You can do it the night before or in the morning. Fill a large bowl about half way with water and add 1/8 cup of salt. Stir. Place chicken pieces in the bowl and set in a refrigerator for at least 4 hours. Water should cover the chicken.

2 cups **flour** seasoned with 1 tablespoon of **salt** and **pepper** and a dash of cayenne

1 stick of **margarine** (8 ounces / 1/2 pound)

(**optional**) chicken-mushroom gravy - 1 can cream of mushroom soup, some **milk**

DIRECTIONS:

1. If you do not brine the chicken, just be sure to run the pieces under cold water and place on a plate with paper towels. If you can, use some kitchen scissors and clip off those little wing tips that are inedible. The wing will lie flatter and brown better. **Pat chicken dry.**

2. Put the seasoned flour in a large baggie or a small paper bag. Put 1 or 2 pieces of chicken in the bag and shake for about 10 seconds. Remove to a clean plate. When finished, put the margarine in the baking dish and put in the 450°F pre-heated oven. When the margarine has melted and starts to sizzle remove it from the oven. Keep an eye on it - do not let it burn. Place chicken in the dish skin side down.

3. Set timer for 25 minutes. Remove, turn chicken over and bake for 20 to 25 more minutes. If you are baking only chicken breasts 20 minutes per side is plenty as they tend to dry out. Remove from oven and place on paper towel.

CHICKEN-MUSHROOM GRAVY

You can make a simple gravy with the melted margarine. If you used a whole chicken or just thighs the margarine has enough chicken flavor. If you used only wings you will need to bump up the chicken flavor with a **dissolved chicken cube** added to the below.

Scrape the dish to loosen all the browned bits. Put 3 tablespoons of the **melted margarine** and **browned bits** in a medium size pot. Add a can of **cream of mushroom soup**. Stir to blend on medium high heat. When it begins to bubble add some **milk**. Add enough milk to make it the consistency you want your gravy, but it should not be thin. Let it cook a few minutes. It's good on mashed potatoes or rice.

EASY ROAST CHICKEN

A roasted chicken is a simple dish, but not short on flavor. You will have leftovers for another meal or two. You may roast a whole chicken, but it **might be easier** to buy a whole chicken cut up or just several pieces of the parts you like which means you will not have to carve it apart when finished and it cooks in half the time. Both recipes are below. *You will obviously have leftover chicken if you roast a whole one. Just pull the meat off the bone, freeze and use in another dish that calls for some cooked chicken. If you roast pieces, cook extra so you have leftovers to freeze and use in other recipes.*

Time: 2 hours   **Servings:** 2-4
Tools: roasting pan for whole chicken or baking dish for pieces.

INGREDIENTS:

1, 3-1/2 to 4 pounds **roasting chicken or a whole chicken cut up,** thawed if frozen

Rub: mix together the following

1 tablespoon of **kosher salt**

1/2 tablespoon ground black **pepper**

1 tablespoon **dried thyme**

1 teaspoon **dried sage**

2 **garlic** cloves minced

1/4 cup oil or olive oil

(option) 1 **lemon,** quartered (for whole chicken only)

In the Roasting Pan: add the items below to the pan. This is optional, but if you are making a gravy it adds a lot of flavor and if you don't have a wire roasting rack placing the chicken on top of the ingredients below keeps the chicken from sitting in it's fat and juices while roasting.

1 large **yellow onion,** thickly sliced

4 **carrots** cut into 2-inch chunks

3 ribs of **celery** cut into 2-inch chunks

Olive oil

DIRECTIONS: WHOLE CHICKEN

1. Preheat oven to 475°F. **Remove the chicken giblets** (neck, heart, liver, gizzard) if they are included with the chicken. They are found in the breast cavity, perhaps in a bag. (Many a novice cook has failed to remove these chicken parts when roasting a chicken.)

2. Rinse the chicken inside and out under cold tap water. Remove any excess fat and leftover pin feathers and pat the outside dry with paper towel. Liberally spread the rub all over the outside and inside of the chicken. Stuff the cavity with the lemon. Tie the legs together (whole chicken) with kitchen string and tuck the wing tips under the body of the chicken. Place the onions, carrots, and celery in the roasting pan. Toss with salt, pepper and a little olive oil. Spread them around the bottom of the roasting pan and place the chicken on top, breast up or on a wire rack if your roasting pan has one.

3. Roast the chicken until the skin begins to brown — 25-30 minutes. Reduce heat to 350°F and continue to roast until an instant-read thermometer inserted into the thigh registers 165°F, approximately 45 to 60 minutes longer or until the juices run clear if you cut between where the thigh and breast meet. If you see pinkish liquid when you cut between the thigh and the breast the chicken is not done.

4. Remove the chicken to a platter and discard the vegetables. If making a gravy pour liquid into a gravy separator. Cover chicken with foil and let sit for 10-15 minutes.
   See **Gravies** *if you want to make a gravy.*

DIRECTIONS: CHICKEN PIECES
Rinse chicken under cold running water and pat dry. Spread oil or butter over all sides of the chicken pieces, then salt and pepper. Place in a baking dish skin side up and bake at 450°F for 45 to 50 minutes.

Chicken Fingers are traditionally deep-fried, but in this recipe you will bake them and get pretty much the same results without all of the oil. You can buy packages of "tenders" at the market — the rib portion of the breast, but they are expensive compared to buying whole boneless, skinless chicken breasts which will work just as well. Chicken Fingers are usually eaten with a dipping sauce like Ranch dressing, blue cheese dressing, horseradish cream (my favorite), or a warmed salsa.

You don't have to make "fingers" with this recipe. You can just use the whole boneless, skinless chicken breast as is. It will take a little longer to cook, however. Just drizzle some lemon juice over it when serving or a have a dipping sauce like Ranch dressing or Horseradish.

Popcorn Chicken Salad: Chicken Fingers are great if after you bake them you slice them in bite size pieces and add them to a nice big salad. All you need is some good bread and you have a good meal.

Time: 45 minutes
Servings: 1
Tools: dredging station, sheet pan
Serve with: Home Fries, potato salad, slaw, green beans

INGREDIENTS:

1 **boneless, skinless chicken breast** cut in 3 portions length-wise - 3 "strips"

cooking spray (like Pam)

"Breading Stations"

See Breading and Frying, page 26.

1/2 cup **flour** mixed with 1 teaspoon **salt and pepper**

1 **egg** beaten with 1 tablespoon of **milk**

1 cup **Panko breadcrumbs**. Panko crumbs make an extra crispy crust. You can substitute plain breadcrumbs or cornflake crumbs.

DIRECTIONS:

Preheat oven to 400°F.

1. Dip a tender in the plain flour to coat and shake off excess.

2. Now dip it into the egg to coat.

3. Now roll it in the panko crumbs, pressing them onto the tender.

4. Place the tender on a baking sheet. Repeat for remaining tenders.

5. When all the tenders are on the baking sheet give them a quick spray with the cooking spray, turn them over and give the other side a quick spray.

6. Bake for 25-30 minutes until done and browned. Turn once half-way through cooking.

Horseradish dipping sauce: 1/4 cup mayonnaise and 1/2 tablespoon of prepared horseradish mixed together.

CHEESECAKE

There are all kinds of cheesecakes. I have several recipes, but this is a good go-to recipe that is very simple and makes a good cheesecake. **You must have a springform pan.** I have never been fond of graham cracker crusts so I buy a package of **butter cookies**. I really think they make a tastier crust. It's up to you. To make it lower fat you can substitute Neufchâtel cheese or low-fat cream cheese, but a cheesecake is for a special occasion — use the good stuff!

Time: 90 minutes
Tools: springform pan, deep baking pan like a broiler pan or roasting pan

INGREDIENTS:

2 packages **cream cheese** placed in a medium size mixing bowl and left to soften (30 minutes)

1 cup **sugar**

1/2 teaspoon **vanilla extract**

3 large **eggs**

8 ounces **sour cream**

1 tablespoon **lemon zest**

Crust:

1-1/2 cups **graham cracker crumbs** or butter cookie crumbs. You can make them in a blender or food processor.

6 tablespoons of **melted butter**

1/2 teaspoon **cinnamon**

1. In a small mixing bowl add two-thirds of the melted butter to the crumbs and cinnamon and mix with a fork. You want them to hold together. Press with a fork. If they hold their shape you don't need to add any more butter. If they are still a little loose add more butter.

2. Pour the crumbs around the bottom of the springform pan with a little extra near the edge. Use your fingers or the flat bottom of a measuring cup to press them down to form a 1/4 inch crust. You want to work them up the side about 1 inch as well. Pack tightly. Place the pan in the fridge.

DIRECTIONS:

1. **Make the crust.**

2. Set one oven rack in the middle of the oven and another rack just below it. Fill a broiler pan or roasting pan with an inch of water and set it in the middle on the lower rack. Preheat oven to 325°F.

3. With a hand blender on low, whip the cream cheese just until smooth. Add 1 egg at a time and beat on low until just incorporated. You don't want to overbeat as that will add air. Now add the sugar, sour cream, vanilla and lemon zest. Beat until just incorporated on low speed.

4. Take the pan out of the fridge. Pour the mixture into the pan and gently jiggle it to even it out. Place a sheet of foil under the pan and wrap it up the sides of the pan.

5. Place the cake pan on the middle rack above the pan that has water in it.

6. Bake for 45 to 55 minutes. At 45 minutes give the cake pan a slight jiggle. The cake is done if only the center is still a little jiggly. *It will firm up when refrigerated.* If the whole cake jiggles, cook for 10 more minutes.

7. When done, turn off the heat. Leave the cake in the oven for 30 minutes **with the door open** about half way.

8. Remove from oven and let it cool for 1 hour on the counter. Place it in the fridge. After another hour cover it with plastic wrap and refrigerate for at least 4 hours. (If you cover it with plastic wrap before it is completely cooled it will sweat.)

9. When ready to serve, run a knife around the inside rim to loosen the crust. Open the latch on the springform pan. Leave the cake on the bottom plate of the pan.

CHESS PIE

This is the easiest pie on the planet - but it's rich and decadent. A great pie to make when you are in a hurry and need something pronto.

Time: 1 hour
Servings: 8
Tools: pie plate, mixing bowl, whisk

INGREDIENTS:

unbaked pie shell

1 stick **butter**

3 **eggs**

1-1/2 cups **sugar**

1 tablespoon **cornmeal**

1 tablespoon **vinegar**

1 teaspoon **vanilla**

(optional) 2 teaspoons of lemon juice and and 2 teaspoons of lemon zest - *I like this addition as it cuts the sweetness and adds a nice lemony touch*

DIRECTIONS:

Preheat oven to 350°F.

1. Melt butter, pour into a mixing bowl and let it cool.

2. Add eggs and sugar. Beat well. Add remainder of ingredients and mix well. Pour into pie shell.

3. Bake for 40 minutes. Check for doneness with a toothpick that when inserted comes out clean.

Decadent Chocolate Cake

When you need to make something special for a group nothing is better than chocolate. This is one of my concoctions — a chocolate cake made with brownie batter. This recipe uses a pre-made mix. You can easily make your own brownies and frosting from scratch — which would be healthier. Instead of the raspberry preserves you can just use frosting to top the first layer.

Time: 2 hours
Servings: 8 - 10
Tools: 2 round cake pans, mixing bowl, hand blender

INGREDIENTS:

1 box of **brownie mix** (the box will say **"Family Size"** for a 9 inch by 13 inch baking dish) — use any variety of brownie mix — double fudge is my favorite. (You will also need **vegetable oil** and **eggs**.) SEE NOTE.

1 jar of **seedless raspberry preserves**

1 container of a store-brand **chocolate frosting** or use recipe below

Simple Chocolate Frosting:

3 1/2 cups **confectioners' sugar**

1 cup unsweetened **cocoa powder**

12 tablespoons (1-1/2 sticks) **unsalted butter, room temperature**

1/2 cup **milk, room temperature**

2 teaspoons pure **vanilla extract**

Directions:
In a small bowl, whisk together the confectioners' sugar and cocoa powder. Add butter, milk and vanilla; stir until smooth and free of lumps.

DIRECTIONS:

NOTE: If you cannot find "Family Size" brownie mix you can buy 2 boxes of brownie mix that use a 9 inch by 9 inch baking dish. See back of box — it will tell you which size pan to use. You can mix the 2 boxes together or mix them separately when preparing them.

Preheat oven according to brownie mix package.

1. Prepare 2 round cake pans: grease bottoms of pans with butter or margarine — only the bottoms. Do not grease the sides of the pans or the brownies will stick to the sides.

2. Mix the batter in a large bowl according to package directions.

3. Divide the batter between the 2 cake pans and bake per package directions. When done, as soon as you take them out of the oven, take a knife and run it around the edges of the pans to make sure the brownies are not stuck to the sides of the pans.

4. Let brownies cool completely, then turn one out onto a plate with the bottom of the brownies facing up - the flattest side. Spread raspberry preserves over top to about 1/4 inch thick.

5. Turn out the second layer. Place the flat side (the bottom) on top of the preserves. Spread icing over top of the layer about 1/4 inch thick.

6. Sprinkle the top with some chopped pecans if you have them.

FRUIT CRISP

A pretty simple dessert, but very tasty with a scoop of ice cream or some whipped cream. You can use apples, pears or fresh peaches, but pears and peaches should be just shy of ripe.

Time: 45 minutes
Servings: 2 - 3
Tools: mixing bowl, small baking dish

INGREDIENTS:

3 large **apples or 4 large peaches or pears** peeled, cored and cut into 3/4 inch cubes (you need about 3 cups of fruit).

Topping:

3/4 cup **flour**

1 cup **sugar**

1/4 pound of **cold butter** (1 stick) cut into small pieces

1/2 teaspoon **cinnamon**

1/4 teaspoon **salt**

1/8 cup chopped **pecans** or walnuts

(optional) 1/4 cup **oatmeal**

DIRECTIONS:

Preheat oven to 400°F.

1. Place fruit in the bottom of a small baking dish greased with butter. Add 2 tablespoons of flour and mix to coat the fruit.

2. In another bowl stir the topping ingredients together just to blend. Then use your clean fingers to mush the mixture together and work the butter into the dry ingredients until you have a coarse mixture and there is no loose flour. You don't want it to be smooth but coarse and chunky.

3. Spread topping on fruit. Bake for 30 minutes or until the topping is browned.

FRUIT GALETTE

A "galette" is a rustic, free form pie, but you do not use a pie plate. The edges are folded up over the fruit and the center of the pie is open. It's very French! N'est pas? See some fruit variations using pears, peaches or strawberries below.

Time: 45 minutes
Servings: 6
Tools: baking sheet lined with parchment paper or a non-stick baking sheet

INGREDIENTS:	DIRECTIONS:
1 unbaked **pie shell**	Preheat oven to 450°F.
3 or 4 large (4 cups) Granny Smith or Golden Delicious **apples**, peeled, cored, cut into 1/8-inch-thick slices	1. Place the room-temperature unbaked crust on a piece of parchment paper on a rimmed baking sheet.
4 tablespoons **sugar**, divided	2. Combine apple slices, 2 tablespoons sugar, flour and lemon peel in medium bowl; toss to blend. *You can't let fruit like apples or pears sit too long before baking or they will begin to turn brown.*
1 tablespoon **cornstarch** or flour	
1 teaspoon finely **grated lemon peel**	3. Spread preserves with a pastry brush over the crust to within 1-1/2 inches of the outer edge of the crust.
1 teaspoon **lemon juice**	4. Arrange apple slices in concentric circles atop preserves, overlapping slightly to within 1-1/2 inches of the outer edge of the crust.
1/4 cup **apricot preserves**	
milk or egg wash (1 egg beaten with 1 tablespoon of water)	5. Fold the 1-1/2 inch crust border up over apples, pinching any cracks in the crust. There will overlapping of crust and that's OK. Brush the crust with egg wash. Sprinkle crust edges and apples with the remaining 2 tablespoons sugar.
	6. Bake for 20 minutes. Reduce oven temperature to 375°F and continue baking until crust is golden, about 30 minutes longer. Remove from oven.
	7. Slide a long thin knife between parchment and galette and move it to a plate or cooling rack if you have one. Let stand at least 10 minutes. Cut into wedges and serve.

VARIATIONS:

• Use pears or peaches instead of apples, but you don't want them to be very ripe, just shy of ripe.

• Use strawberries cut in half and use strawberry preserves instead of apricot.

Rum Cake

A simple, easy, rich bundt cake. The recipe allows for many delicious variations.

Tools: greased bundt pan or angel food cake pan, hand mixer,
measuring cups, large mixing bowl, spatula, small sauce pan
Oven Temp: 350°F

INGREDIENTS:

Cake Batter:

1 box **Yellow Cake Mix**

1 regular package **French Vanilla Instant pudding** (3.4 oz)

1/2 cup canola or vegetable **oil**

1/2 cup **water**

1/2 cup **rum**

4 **eggs**

Topping:
1 cup chopped **pecans**

Sauce:
1 cup **sugar**
1/4 cup **water**
1/2 cup **rum**
1/2 stick **butter**

DIRECTIONS:

1. Grease a bundt pan with butter and dust with flour: sprinkle 3 tablespoons of flour into the pan and keep turning the pan and moving the pan until the flour has coated the butter. Invert pan and tap to remove excess flour.

2. Place nuts in an even layer in the bottom of bundt pan.

3. Put all batter ingredients in a large mixing bowl. Beat on low speed for 1 minute. Use a spatula to scrape sides and bottom of bowl. Then beat on medium speed for 2 more minutes. Pour batter evenly into bundt pan. Jiggle it to help even it out.

Bake for 35 to 45 minutes. (test doneness with a knife - insert a thin blade into the center, if knife comes out clean it's done, if gooey it needs to cook a few more minutes.)

SAUCE:
After the cake is done melt butter in a small sauce pan, then add rest of ingredients, Simmer 3 minutes. Keep it on warm until you are ready to use so the butter doesn't congeal. After cake has been out of the oven for 20 minutes, pour the warm sauce over cake. Let sit for an hour or more to cool then invert the cake onto a plate.

VARIATIONS:

ORANGE CAKE:
Same as **Rum Cake** above, but: substitute orange juice for rum and water and add a couple tablespoons of orange zest to batter.

CHOCOLATE-ORANGE CAKE
Same as **Rum Cake** above, but: substitute a box of any kind of chocolate cake mix (chocolate fudge, etc.) and a box of chocolate instant pudding; substitute orange juice for rum in the batter and orange juice for rum and water in the sauce; add a couple of tablespoons of orange zest to batter.

LEMON CAKE:
Same as **Rum Cake** above, but: substitute Lemon Cake Mix, lemon juice for rum in the sauce and water for the rum in the batter, add 2 tablespoons lemon zest to batter.

BANANAS FOSTER

Actually, I'm not sure if this is an authentic recipe for Bananas Foster! I just know it's similar and it tastes really good over ice cream or a slice of plain pound cake or pancakes or French toast.

Time: 5 minutes
Servings: 1
Tools: small skillet

INGREDIENTS:	DIRECTIONS:
1 **banana** *(don't slice it until you are ready to add it to the pan or it may turn brown)*	1. Melt the butter in a small skillet on medium-high heat. Add the brown sugar and rum and stir until the sugar has melted into the butter and the mixture is bubbling. (Add cream and mix in.)
2 tablespoons **butter**	
1/8 cup **dark brown sugar** (packed into the measuring cup). You can use light brown sugar if that's all you have.	2. Reduce heat to medium. Cut banana into 1/2 inch rounds and toss them and the pecans into the pan. Cook for 1 minute stirring often. Don't overcook or the bananas become too mushy.
1 tablespoon **rum or bourbon** or water	3. You're done. How easy was that?
1 tablespoon **chopped pecans** or walnuts	
(optional) 2 tablespoons **heavy cream**	

BAKED ZITI

Baked ziti is very similar to lasagna. It's the same ingredients, but mixed in a different way and a bit less work.

Time: 1 hour (if you have a marinara/meat sauce prepared in advance
or use a jar brand.)
Servings: 2 - 3
Tools: 9" by 9" baking dish or medium size casserole dish, large mixing bowl,
pot for cooking pasta

INGREDIENTS:

1 carton **ricotta** cheese (16 ounces - low fat, part skim or whole milk)

1/2 cup **parmesan** cheese

2 cups (16 ounces) cubed **mozzarella** cheese (the size of a sugar cube)

1 tsp **salt**

1/4 cup. chopped fresh **parsley**

1 **egg**

6 ounces (1/3 box) **ziti pasta** cooked according to box instructions (Ziti is a short, hollow tubular pasta. You could also use a small penne pasta.)

4 cups **meat sauce** (You can make your own – see *Quick Marinara recipe* – or buy 2 jars of a marinara and add 1 pound of cooked and drained of its fat ground beef, ground mild italian sausage or ground pork and simmer together for at least 30 minutes.)

DIRECTIONS:

1. Preheat oven to 450°F.

2. Cook and drain the pasta.

3. In a large mixing bowl, mix together the ricotta, parmesan, parsley, salt and egg. Now add the cooked pasta and mix well.

4. Make a layer using 1/3 of the ricotta-coated noodles. Sprinkle the layer with 1/3 of your cubed mozzarella. Pour 1/3 of your sauce over the noodles and spread it around. Repeat to make 3 layers.

5. Add a little extra parmesan to the top of the last layer.

6. Place in the oven on a foil-lined cookie sheet (to catch any boil-over mess) and turn down the temperature to 400°F. Bake for 30 to 45 minutes, more or less, until it looks "set" and not runny. Let it cool for at least 15 minutes covered with foil before serving so it can "set up."

FETTUCCINE ALFREDO

This is a fast, simple, tasty, dish but very rich. There are 2 recipes – a **classic version** which is high in fat due to the cream and a **lite version**. It won't kill you to enjoy the classic recipe occasionally! You could also add some mushrooms, broccoli or asparagus — see *Variations* and **PASTA PRIMAVERA** at bottom.

Time: 30 minutes
Servings: 1
Tools: pot for cooking pasta, large sauté pan.

INGREDIENTS: *CLASSIC VERSION*	DIRECTIONS:
4 ounces (1/3 box) **fettuccine pasta** (regular or spinach)	1. Boil the pasta according to directions.
4 ounces **heavy cream**	2. Once the pasta is cooking put the cream in a medium skillet with nutmeg. Bring to a slight simmer.
1/2 cup **parmesan cheese**	3. When the pasta is done scoop it out of the water and place in the skillet. **Reserve the pasta water**. Add 1/4 cup of the reserved pasta water to the pan. Simmer the pasta in the cream for 3 minutes. Remove pan from heat. Stir in parmesan cheese and parsley - this will thicken it. The pasta should be creamy when you eat it and cream thickens as it cools so if it looks a little thick or dry after you have stirred in the parmesan add some of the **hot pasta water** to thin it. Serve in a warmed bowl.
2 tablespoon **fresh chopped parsley**	
1/8 teaspoon of ground **nutmeg**	
1/2 cup **reserved pasta water**	
INGREDIENTS: *LITE VERSION*	
Substitute the following for whole cream:	
2 heaping tablespoons **lite sour cream**	
1/2 cup **milk**	

Variations:

Sometimes you will see this dish served with slices of **grilled chicken** mixed in with the pasta. You can grill some chicken or sauté it in another pan and slice it up. Add it to the pasta when you put it in the skillet.

You could also add sliced **mushrooms** (crimini or portabellas) that you have sautéed in a little butter until golden brown.

To make this a **PASTA PRIMAVERA** use only 2 ounces of cream and add 1/3 cup of chicken broth; add any or all of the following: thinly sliced cooked carrots, broccoli, zucchini, peas, asparagus and mushrooms which have been steamed or cooked just to tender.

Lasagna recipes are usually made in a large 9" x 13" baking pan/dish which makes 6 to 8 servings. While you can freeze uneaten portions you may not want several servings languishing in your freezer for months. This recipe uses a bread pan that makes 2 servings.

Time: 1 hour (if you have a marinara/meat sauce prepared in advance
or use a jar brand.)
Servings: 2
Tools: a loaf pan, mixing bowl, pot for cooking pasta

INGREDIENTS:

1 carton **ricotta cheese** (16 ounces - low fat, part skim or whole milk)

1/2 cup **parmesan cheese plus 1/4 cup** for topping.

2 cups (16 ounces) shredded or thinly sliced **mozzarella cheese**

1 tsp **salt**

1/4 cup. chopped **fresh parsley**

1 **egg**

4 **lasagna noodles** (You can use the no-boil variety which are flat, not curly or the regular kind that you cook in advance. If you use the kind that need to be cooked, only cook them for 1/2 the time suggested on the box. They will cook to doneness in the lasagna. The advantage of the no-boil noodle is that it makes it super easy to spread the ricotta cheese mixture.)

4 cups (32 ounces) **meat sauce** (You can make your own - see *Quick Marinara* recipe - or buy 2 jars of a marinara and add 1 pound of cooked and drained of its fat ground beef, ground mild italian sausage or ground pork and simmer together for at least 30 minutes.)

DIRECTIONS:

1. Preheat oven to 450°F.

2. In a medium mixing bowl, mix together the ricotta, 1/2 cup parmesan, parsley and egg.

3. Have your meat sauce and noodles ready.

4. Put a couple of tablespoons of your sauce in the bottom of the loaf pan and spread to coat the bottom. If you use no-boil noodles, gingerly spread 1/4 of the ricotta mixture on the noodle with a knife like you are buttering a slice of bread then put it in the pan. Be careful not to break the noodle. If you use a cooked noodle, place it in the pan and drop 1/4 cup of the ricotta mixture in small dollops evenly over the noodle.

5. Sprinkle the ricotta-topped noodle with 1/4 of the shredded mozzarella or cover it with thin slices.

6. Now pour 1/4 of your sauce (about 1/2 cup) on top of the cheese.

7. Now repeat: noodle, ricotta, mozzarella, meat sauce. Each time you add a noodle press it down slightly to compact it. Add parmesan to the top of the last layer.

8. Cover the dish with foil and place in the oven on a foil-lined cookie sheet (to catch any boil-over mess) and turn down the temperature to 400°F. Remove foil on top when it starts to bubble. Bake for 45 minutes, more or less, until it looks "set" and not runny. Let it cool for at least 15 minutes covered with foil before serving so it can "set up."

PASTA WITH OLIVE OIL & GARLIC

This is a classic, fast, simple, light, tasty dish. The actual Italian name is *Aglio at Oilio*. I have added vegetables to make it a complete dish. **If you have access to an Italian grocery or deli** they may have in-store made frozen pastas like tortellini or ravioli. These also work well with this recipe.

Time: 15 minutes
Serving: 1
Tools: pot for cooking pasta, large non-stick sauté pan.

INGREDIENTS:

1/4 to 1/3 of a 1 pound box of **pasta** – spaghetti, angel hair, ziti, penne, fettuccine (regular or spinach). If using ravioli or tortellini you got frozen from an Italian market, use a serving amount.

1/4 cup **extra virgin olive** oil plus 2 tablespoons for finishing the dish

1 tablespoon of **butter**

several cloves of **garlic** peeled and smashed (use as much garlic as you like!)

1 tablespoon fresh chopped **parsley**

1/3 cup **parmesan** cheese

1/2 cup reserved **pasta water**

2 slices of cooked **bacon** crumbled or some thinly sliced chopped ham or pancetta

(*optional*) 1 cup of bit size **vegetables** - either broccoli, peas, cauliflower (my favorite), Brussels sprouts or asparagus or a mixture of any you like.

DIRECTIONS:

If you do not use the optional bacon move on to Step 2.

1. If you use the bacon, fry it, drain it and when cooled, crumble it. Leave 1 tablespoon of the bacon fat in the pan and discard the rest. Go to Step 2, adding the olive oil to the skillet with the bacon fat.

2. Heat the olive oil in the pan on medium heat. Add garlic. Reduce heat to low. Sauté the garlic for 5 minutes on the low heat to infuse the oil. Do not burn the garlic! Turn off the heat. Remove the garlic (unless you want to eat it which is good because now it is mild.) Add the butter.

3. Boil the pasta in salted water according to directions. (If you are adding vegetables add them to the pasta in the last 3 minutes. If adding very thin asparagus see Step 4.) You can steam the vegetables separately, but why dirty another pot when you have some boiling water already going?

4. When the pasta (and vegetables are done) save 1 cup of the pasta water and drain the pasta. Put the pasta (and vegetables and ham or bacon) in the skillet, return to medium heat and add 1/4 cup of the pasta water. (Now is the time to add the thin asparagus.) Simmer for 3 minutes, stirring often. Remove from heat, add parmesan, parsley, fresh ground pepper and drizzle with 2 tablespoons of olive oil.

Serve in a warmed bowl with extra parmesan cheese.

This marinara sauce is intended for use with Italian casseroles like lasagna, stuffed shells or baked ziti. It is basically the same as the recipe for the marinara given in the recipe for Spaghetti and Meatballs, but with less water and a shorter cooking time. It doesn't need to cook as long since it will be cooking in the oven in the casserole and baking enhances flavor more than simmering on a stove. If making the 2-serving lasagna recipe or the baked ziti recipe you will not need the full amount. Just freeze any remaining unused sauce. *And by the way... it's a lot better than any brand you buy in a jar!*

Time: 30-60 minutes
Tools: 6 quart pot, large skillet if browning meat for a meat sauce

INGREDIENTS: MARINARA	DIRECTIONS:
1/8 cup **olive oil**	1. In a large 6 quart pot add oil, onions and garlic. Sauté on low heat until translucent (do not let the onions brown), stir often. Takes about 15 minutes.
3 cups diced **onions**	
4 to 6 large **garlic cloves** peeled	
1, large (28 ounces) can **crushed tomatoes** (use *Cento* brand if you can find it.)	2. Add the rest of the ingredients and mix well.
1, 12 oz. can **tomato paste**	3. Simmer covered for 30 to 60 minutes. You will need to stir the sauce about every 15 minutes.
1 teaspoon **salt**	
1 teaspoon ground black **pepper**	
1 teaspoon **sugar**	
1/2 teaspoon **red pepper flakes**	
1 tablespoon **dried oregano**	
1 cup **water**	

MEAT SAUCE:
Add to the above: 1 pound **ground beef** or 1/2 pound of **ground beef** and 1/2 pound of **ground pork** that has been browned in a skillet and well-drained. Add this after you have added the tomatoes to the sautéed onions. You could also use all or some **ground Italian sausage** (mild, not hot) instead. Sausage makes for a spicier marinara.

RAGOUT SAUCE
A ragout sauce is a chunkier sauce because of added vegetables. You will add the following ingredients to the onions and sauté: 1 cup finely chopped **celery**, 1 cup finely chopped **carrots**. If you want it to be a meat sauce add meat as described for Meat Sauce above.

Spaghetti alla Carbonara

This classic dish is traditionally made with pancetta, an Italian bacon/ham-like product. Since that is not always so easy to find you will see this recipe often made with bacon as it is here. Add vegetables to make a one-pot meal. See NOTE at bottom.

Time: 20 minutes
Servings: 1
Tools: medium pot to cook pasta, large skillet

INGREDIENTS:

1/4 to 1/3 pound dry **spaghetti** (a single serving) boiled in 3 cups of water

2 **eggs at room temperature**

2 or 3 strips of fried and crumbled **bacon**

1/3 cup freshly grated good **parmesan cheese or pecorino romano**

Freshly cracked black **pepper**

1 tablespoon fresh chopped **parsley**

salt to taste

(optional) broccoli, peas or asparagus - see Note below.

FYI: The pasta is cooked in half the usual amount of water in order to have a much starchier water that is used to thicken and moisten the carbonara.

DIRECTIONS:

This dish must be made quickly since you don't cook the ingredients together. The mixture is poured over hot pasta and it is done. If the pasta is luke warm this dish does not work.

1. Fry the bacon to almost crisp – it should still have a bit of chew. Remove, drain and chop coarsely.

2. While the bacon is frying whisk the eggs, cheese, pepper and parsley in a small bowl until well-combined.

3. Bring 3 cups of generously salted water to a boil, add the spaghetti and cook according to package directions. (See note below.) When the pasta is done, reserve 1/2 cup of the water in a measuring cup, then drain quickly and immediately return the pasta to the pot, but off the heat.

4. **While whisking constantly slowly drizzle** 1/4 cup of the reserved hot pasta water into the egg mixture. Immediately add the egg mixture to the pasta, and with a pair of tongs toss the pasta for about 1 minute. The residual heat will cook the eggs but work quickly to prevent the eggs from scrambling. If the sauce seems too thick, thin it out with a little bit more of the reserved pasta water. It should be very creamy.

5. Taste for salt. Add fresh parsley. Add more parmesan if you like on top when serving.

NOTE: I often add broccoli or peas or sliced asparagus to this dish so I have a vegetable that I don't have to cook in another pot. Just add them to the pasta water in the last 3 minutes to cook with the pasta.

STUFFED SHELLS

This recipe makes a lot of shells – there is no way to make a smaller amount without wasting a lot of ingredients. With a simple marinara this is a meatless meal. Figure 3 to 4 shells per person. *You can freeze serving portions.*

Time: 90 minutes (if you have a marinara or meat sauce already prepared)
Servings: 6 to 8
Tools: 2, 9' by 13" baking dishes, large mixing bowl,
large pot for boiling pasta shells.

INGREDIENTS:

FILLING:

1 carton **ricotta cheese** (12 oz)

1/2 cup **parmesan** cheese

1 cup shredded **mozzarella** cheese

1 tsp **salt**

1/4 cup chopped fresh **parsley**

1 **egg**

(optional, but highly recommended)
1 package **frozen chopped spinach** thawed and squeezed dry – *wad it into a ball and squeeze it between your palms over and over until no liquid comes out.*

PASTA:

24 **jumbo pasta shells** - 18 if you do not use spinach in the filling (Always cook a few extra shells as a few will tear while cooking and not be usable.)

SAUCE:

8 to 10 cups **Marinara or Meat Sauce** — *see NOTE below*

DIRECTIONS:

1. Mix all the filling ingredients in a large bowl.

2. Boil shells in salted water for about 8 minutes, stirring often so they do not stick, not the full time as you want them pliable but not soft - they tend to tear the longer they are cooked. They will cook to tender when they are baked in the sauce. Drain shells and rinse with cold water just enough so you can handle them. You want to stuff them before they cool down and start sticking to one another.

3. Put a little sauce in the bottom of the baking dish. Fill each shell with a heaping tablespoon of the filling. Fold the shell closed. Place them in the dish leaving about 1 inch between them (12 shells will fit into a 9"x13" dish) and then pour 4 to 5 cups of your sauce over them. (Do not overcrowd them as they will swell while cooking. If you have too many shells freeze them.) Sprinkle top with extra shredded mozzarella and some parmesan cheese.

4. Bake at 400°F covered until the sauce starts to bubble, then uncover and bake for about 30 minutes at 350°F. Let rest for about 10 minutes before serving.

NOTE: You can prepare the casseroles in advance and put them in the fridge, covered, until you are ready to bake them. It will take them longer to start bubbling if you do this unless you let them come to room temperature before you bake them.

NOTE: If you make or have a frozen batch of the marinara or meat sauce from the recipe in this book you can use that. Just thaw and warm in a pot. You can make a quick marinara or meat sauce by using a large can or jar of a prepared marinara, but avoid Ragu and Prego! Get one with garlic and onion. Put it in a large pot with 1, large (28 ounces) can of crushed tomatoes, a 6 ounce can of tomato paste and 1 cup of water. Add 1 teaspoon of salt. If you want a meat sauce fry up a pound of hamburger or ground pork (or ground turkey if you so choose) and add it to the sauce. Simmer for 30 minutes.

Everything you see I owe to spaghetti.
SOPHIA LOREN

The Marinara Sauce

There is nothing more classic than this dish. A good marinara (spaghetti sauce) takes time - several hours. So make it on a day you will be at home!

I never make a single batch, though this recipe is for a single batch. I like to freeze half of a double batch of the sauce for use later for a lasagna, stuffed shells or a baked ziti. A single batch of this sauce and meatballs will make enough for 4 to 5 meals.

If you freeze a second batch of marinara you can always add some meat to it later when you thaw it out to make a meat sauce for a lasagna, stuffed shells or a baked ziti. Freeze it in 1 or 2 cup portions.

Time: 4 to 5 hours   **Servings:** 4 to 5
Tools: 6 quart pot or larger

INGREDIENTS: MARINARA	DIRECTIONS:
1/8 cup **olive oil** 3 cups diced yellow **onions** 4 to 6 large **garlic cloves**, finely chopped 1, large (28 ounces) can **crushed tomatoes** (use *Cento* brand if you can find it.) 1, 12 oz. can **tomato paste** 1 teaspoon **salt** 1 teaspoon ground black **pepper** 1 teaspoon **sugar** 1/2 teaspoon. **red pepper flakes** 1 tablespoon **dried oregano** 2 cups **water**	1. In a large 6 quart pot add oil, onions and garlic. Sauté on low heat until translucent (do not let the onions brown), stir often. Takes about 15 minutes. 2. Add the rest of the ingredients and mix well. 3. Simmer covered for 4 or more hours. Remove the lid to let the sauce thicken for the last hour of cooking. You will need to **stir the sauce about every 15 minutes.** *RAGOUT MARINARA: a ragout is a chunkier tomato sauce and has a slightly richer flavor. To make a ragout add 1 cup diced celery and 1 cup diced carrot to Step 1 above.*

THE MEATBALLS

Once you have the marinara simmering you can prepare the meatballs. Don't' wait and do them at the end as you want them to cook in the sauce for a few hours. The secret to this recipe is the **seeded rye breadcrumbs** and the amount of breadcrumbs which makes for very tender and moist meatballs.

USES:
1. Serve meatballs and sauce with pasta
2. Use to make a meatball sub (meatballs, provolone or mozzarella cheese and marinara on a sub roll
3. Just eat them on their own with a little sauce, some good bread and a salad.

INGREDIENTS: MEATBALLS	DIRECTIONS:
1/2 pound **ground chuck** 1/2 pound **ground pork** 1-1/2 cups **seeded rye bread breadcrumbs** (make them in a blender using a good rye bread - one that is not too doughy, but a firmer rye bread with caraway seeds. 1/2 cup **plain breadcrumbs** 1 **egg** 1/4 cup **fresh chopped parsley** 1 teaspoon **garlic powder** 1/2 cup **grated parmesan cheese** 1 teaspoon each **salt and pepper**	Mix all ingredients well (just use clean hands) and form into meatballs a little larger than a golf ball. Place on a baking sheet lined with non-stick foil. Bake for 30 minutes at 400°F. Rotate balls half way through cooking. Drain meatballs on paper towel then add to the large pot of simmering marinara sauce. Let them cook for the entire length of the sauce.

THE SPAGHETTI

Use any kind of pasta you like, you don't have to use spaghetti — I prefer vermicelli or angel hair, both thinner than spaghetti. You could also use ziti or penne or rigatoni or mostaccioli.

Cook a serving of pasta according to pasta directions — **do not add oil to the water.** Drain. Place the pasta back in the saucepan and add some marinara sauce, but don't drown it! Heat the pasta and sauce together for 5 minutes. This allows the pasta to absorb the sauce and gives the pasta more flavor than just pouring some sauce on top of it.

LEFTOVERS:
Place a serving of meatballs, 2 or 3, in a small storage carton with about 1 cup of the marinara and freeze as individual servings. Boil some pasta and add to the pot of reheated meatballs and sauce.

EASY SUPER-THIN & CRISPY PIZZA

For the crust you will use mexican tortillas which make for a very thin and crispy crust.

Time: 30 minutes
Servings: 1
Tools: pizza pan or baking sheet

INGREDIENTS:

flour tortillas - any size will do, just use as many as you need for a serving.

some **marinara or pizza sauce**

shredded **mozzarella**

any **toppings** you want - pepperoni, sausage, bell pepper, mushrooms, onion, etc

grated **parmesan**

oregano

caraway seed

DIRECTIONS:

Preheat oven to 425°F.

1. Place your tortilla(s) on the baking sheet or pizza pan and place in oven for 5 minutes - no longer. Remove from oven.

2. Spread some pizza sauce on the tortilla.

3. Add mozzarella. Sprinkle a little dried oregano and some caraway seeds over the cheese. Now add your toppings. Top with a little parmesan. *If adding green peppers I like to add them about 10 minutes before the pizza is done to preserve their bite.* **Be careful not to overdo the cheese and toppings** as the thin crust cannot support a lot of weight! This is a simple, light pizza.

TIP: pepperoni is extremely fatty. If you want to reduce the fat, put the pepperoni on some paper towel on a plate and microwave for 30 to 60 seconds, depending on how much you use. You will be astonished how much fat comes out of the pepperoni. The pepperoni will shrink in size and actually get crispy!

4. Bake at 425°F on the lowest rack in your oven until the edges begin to curl up and turn dark brown - 20-25 minutes.

CHILI

There are scores of recipes for chili. Most people tweak their recipe to fit their taste which is a good thing. Some people like their chili very spicy. Some like it thin and soupy and others like it thick. Some people like to add beans or spaghetti and others don't. Use this recipe as a starting point and make it how you like it. Some recipes take less than an hour to cook, but to really get deep flavor you need to cook it longer than that. True recipes use cubed beef, like chuck or shoulder. You could certainly use that instead, but you will have to cook it a few hours so the beef gets good and tender.

Time: 3 to 4 hours
Servings: 4 to 6 (freeze leftover portions)
Tools: Dutch Oven or 6 quart saucepot

INGREDIENTS:

2 pounds of **ground chuck (OR** a mix of ground chuck and ground turkey or lean ground pork or use all turkey to make it leaner).

1, 14.5 ounce can **crushed tomatoes**

1, 6 ounce can **tomato paste**

1 or 2, 15.5 ounce cans **chili beans** (like *Brook's* - beans in a chili sauce, choose mild or hot; if you like a lot of beans in your chili use 2 cans - beans are the healthiest thing in the chili!)

2 medium **onions** chopped

1, 7 ounce can **diced green chilies**

1, 14 ounce can **beef broth (or 1 bottle of beer or 1-1/2 cups water)**

1/2 tablespoon **oregano**

4 tablespoon of a good "**chili powder**"

2 teaspoons **salt**

DIRECTIONS:

1. In a large pot, brown the meat. Put the meat in a colander or sieve and strain off the grease. Return meat to pot, add onions and continue to cook on medium-high heat until the onions are soft. Stir often. This also adds more browning to the meat which means more flavor.

2. Add everything else in the list **except the beans**. Mix well. Cover and simmer for at least 2 hours stirring occasionally.

3. After 2 hours add the beans. Use the liquid in the beans as well, don't rinse them. Uncover the pot and let it simmer for 30 more minutes or until it reaches the consistency you prefer — thick or thin. Add water to thin if you so desire. Taste it at this point and decide if you want it spicier. If so, add more chili powder or salt if needed. Chili powder tends to cook out so you often need to add more just near the end. If you want spaghetti in your chili, add some cooked spaghetti to your bowl.

CHILI-MAC

Chili meets Mac and Cheese - a good way to turn leftover chili into something more. To a serving of chili in a saucepan add 1 can of diced tomatoes drained and simmer for 15 minutes. Then add 1 cup cooked macaroni and simmer for 10 more minutes. Remove from heat and add 1/2 cup shredded cheddar cheese. Stir in the cheese until melted and serve.

ENCHILADAS

This recipe will work with chicken, beef or pork. Recipe makes 2 flour enchiladas or 4 corn enchiladas. A good way to use any leftover cooked chicken, beef or pork. You can also use cooked hamburger.

Time: 30 minutes (using leftover meat/poultry)
Servings: 2 (save one for leftovers)
Tools: 2 small sauce pots, foil-lined baking sheet or non-stick baking sheet
Serve with: rice and beans

INGREDIENTS:

2, 8 inch **flour tortillas or** 4 of the smaller **corn tortillas**

1 small can (4 oz) **diced green chiles**

2 tablespoons **water**

1 can **tomato sauce**

1 can **salsa verde**

green onions sliced

1 package **taco seasoning**, mild or hot

1 cup shredded **cheddar cheese**

sour cream and/or guacamole for topping

FILLING:

1 cup cooked **shredded or chopped chicken, beef or pork** or cooked ground beef.

DIRECTIONS:

1. In a small pot, mix meat, green chiles, 1/2 of the taco seasoning and water. Simmer10 minutes. *You can add beans (black, pinto, red) to this mixture if you want instead of having them as a side dish. Use about 1/3 of a can.*

2. In another small pot mix tomato sauce and rest of taco seasoning. Simmer 5 minutes

3. Heat oven to 350°F.

4. Place tortillas on the baking sheet and put in oven for 2 minutes to warm and soften. Remove tortillas.

5. Divide the filling among the tortillas. Spread a mound of the meat from one end to the other off to one side. Roll up tortilla and place in the baking dish seam side down.

6. Spoon 2 tablespoons of the tomato sauce mixture over each tortilla. (Freeze remainder for another time.)

7. Bake for 15 minutes. Remove and top tortillas with grated cheddar. Then bake until cheese is melted.

8. Once it is plated, pour some warmed salsa verde over tortillas and sprinkle with some spring onion.

Serve with beans, rice, guacamole, sour cream, chopped tomatoes, shredded lettuce... you know, all that Mexican stuff.

PORK

Your grocery will have an array of pork cuts. Some can be cooked quickly like a thin pork chop or pork cutlets while others like it low-and-slow like ribs, pork shoulder and butt.

Because of current feeding procedures we do not have to worry about trichinosis any longer. Plus, at 137°F. the trichina would be killed which is below the 140°F recommended temperature for cooked pork.

Let's start with two most common pork chops: the **center loin chop or loin chop** and the **pork rib chop**. *NOTE: Your market may have their own names for them!* The center loin chop looks like a T-bone steak — 2 sections of meat with a T-shaped bone running between them. On one side is the loin and the smaller piece in the tenderloin. This is the priciest chop because it has the

tenderloin meat. Tenderloin is very tender and moist whereas the loin tends to be dryer and a little less tender. The rib chop is the center loin chop with the tenderloin removed. A bone always gives a chop more flavor. You will also see some very thick cut rib chops. These are often slit to create a pocket and then stuffed with a stuffing.

You will also see loin chops where the bone is removed. They are just loin meat. They might be

called **cutlets**. They come thin or thick. Sometimes you will see a cut called a **butterfly chop** where they have split a thick loin and folded it open.

Everyone is familiar with ribs, but they too come in different cuts: **spare ribs** (less fat than other ribs), and **baby back** ribs (meatier than spare ribs). There are also **country-style ribs** which are not really ribs at all, but are meatier and fattier (fat is flavor) and come bone-in or boneless. Again, bones are good. All ribs require a low-and-slow cooking method to melt the connective tissue and make them tender. Country-style ribs come as individual pieces not as a rack.

Country-style ribs

The **pork tenderloin** compares to the beef tenderloin from which we get the filet mignon. The pork tenderloin is a long piece of meat with little fat, but is moist and tender and only requires roasting for 30 to 40 minutes. You often see them

in a tight clear plastic package. There are normally two tenderloins in the package though you can't see that.

There are several types of **pork roasts: rib roasts**, top **loin roasts**, **Boston Butts** and **shoulder roasts**, to name a few. Loin roasts are an all white-meat roast with no bone and little fat. If you over cook it the roast is dry and chewy. Butts and shoulders have lots of fat which keeps the

meat moist, but they require longer, slow cooking times up to 6 hours or more. These cuts are often used for pulled pork BBQ.

BBQ Ribs

For this recipe you need a rack of pork ribs - **baby back ribs**, **spare ribs**, or even **country ribs** (see below). A rack is more than a serving. Cook the entire rack and save the uneaten portion for another meal or pull the meat off the bones, chop it up and save it for a pork BBQ sandwiches. This is a "low and slow recipe" (3 hours) which produces fall-off-the-bone ribs.

Time: 3 hours
Servings: 3 to 4
Tools: rimmed cookie sheet or shallow roasting pan,
extra wide aluminum foil
Serve with: slaw, potato salad, twice baked potato, baked sweet potato,
green vegetable, fried apples, baked beans

INGREDIENTS:

1 rack of **ribs** (*see note below for "country-style" ribs)

2 cups of **BBQ sauce** (there's a simple recipe below, or you can use something from a bottle - recommended - KC Masterpiece). *I find bottled sauces too strong and tend to mix them with half ketchup to tone them down.*

BBQ Sauce:
Mix all the ingredients below in a medium saucepan and simmer covered for 30 minutes.

1 cup **ketchup**

1 small can **tomato sauce**

2 teaspoons **worcestershire sauce**

1/2 cup finely chopped **onion** or 2 teaspoons onion powder

2 heaping tablespoons of **brown sugar**

3 teaspoons **apple cider vinegar**

1 teaspoon each of **paprika** and **cumin** or chili powder

(**optional**) a dash of liquid smoke

DIRECTIONS:

1. Set oven to 300°F.

2. Line the bottom of a shallow roasting pan or rimmed cookie sheet with foil and let it extend over the sides about 6 inches. Place the ribs on the foil. Salt and pepper both sides. Be sure the curved side (top of ribs) is facing up when done. Slather both sides with BBQ sauce. Place another piece of foil the same size on top and seal all four sides well. (You could just use foil on top, but using foil on the bottom and creating a "bag" makes for easy clean-up!). Place in oven on middle rack and bake for 3 hours.

3. When done remove ribs to a plate. Be careful as they will want to fall apart. Discard foil and grease in the foil. Place the ribs back on the pan. Slather with more bbq sauce. Place back in oven with broiler on. Broil until the BBQ sauce begins to bubble and brown - 7-10 minutes.

Using "Country-Style" ribs:

These are not really ribs, but the flavor is similar. They come bone in or boneless. It does not matter for this recipe, though anything with bones has more flavor. Cook the same way as above.

Pan-Fried Pork Chops

This is an all-purpose recipe for any type of **pork chop, cutlet** or **butterfly chop.** Personally, I never buy cutlets or butterfly chops. They just don't have the flavor of a center-cut loin chop or rib chop because they lack a bone and bones add flavor and moistness, but you may use whatever you like.

A **1/4** to **1/2 inch thick chop** is perfect for pan-frying. You may see some chops cut about 1/4 inch thick. These are fine, but cook very quickly. You will see some chops about an inch thick. These are best seared in a skillet then finished in the oven or just cooked on a grill. Whatever you do, **don't overcook your chops** or they will get dry and tough.

You can either dredge the chops in flour or bread them with some bread, cracker or cornflake crumbs.

Time: 30 minutes
Serving: 1
Tools: medium or large skillet depending on size and number of chops
Serve with: cooked apples, green vegetable, rice pilaf or buttered boiled new potatoes or some mashed potatoes with cream gravy or packaged pork gravy mix.

INGREDIENTS:	DIRECTIONS:
1 or 2, 1/2 inch chops depending on kind and size — a serving portion flour or bread, cracker or cornflake crumbs for coating salt and pepper	1. Pat the chops dry and dredge them in some flour to which you have added some salt and pepper — or press some type of crumbs into both sides of the chop and sprinkle with salt and pepper. Let rest for 10 minutes. 2. Heat your skillet with a few tablespoons of oil to medium high heat. 3. Place the chop(s) in the pan. Cook for about 3 to 4 minutes on one side. When the edges of the meat begin to look cooked turn the chop and cook for another 3 minutes or so. *(If your chops are thinner than 1/2 inch they will take less time.)* *Serve with a wedge of lemon to squeeze over the chop(s) or make a cream gravy.*

Fried Apples / Applesauce

Cooked apples are perfect with any kind of pork. Peel and core some apples — Golden Delicious variety are my favorite. Cut them in 1/2 inch slices. Toss them in a small saucepan. Add 1 tablespoon of water, some cinnamon, a little sugar or brown sugar. Cover, bring to a boil, reduce to a simmer and cook for 3 minutes. Remove from heat, but leave them in the pot covered. They will continue to cook without getting mushy. If you want **applesauce**, remove cover after 5 minutes and let them cook until all juice is gone then just mash them up.

HAM

Everybody should know how to bake a ham... so here it is. A ham is a lot of food for one person, but a ham can provide you with many meals as it can be frozen in servings, thawed and eaten on a sandwich or added to other recipes like green beans, scrambled eggs, pasta dishes, etc.

There are fresh or preserved hams, country hams and pre-cooked hams. How you cook them is basically the same. You can also enhance the flavor of your ham by using different glazes.

Choose a type of ham: Most hams that you buy at the grocery store are precooked or partially cooked, and now many of them are also pre-sliced (spiral cut) with a package of glaze. If you buying a precooked ham you will save a lot of cooking time. You can buy hams with the bone-in or the bone removed, but bone-in hams are a little more flavorful and you end up with a bone that makes THE best bean soup. Spiral-cut hams are very easy to serve because you do not have to slice them, but might become drier during cooking. Baking them covered with foil can help to allay this.

Always read the label accompanying the ham to determine whether it is fresh or preserved and whether it has or has not been precooked. This information will help you to determine the proper cooking procedures for your ham.

Storing the ham: You must store a ham properly to prevent the growth of bacteria. Keep your ham in refrigerator at a temperature of 40°F or lower. **Boneless ham** can be stored in the refrigerator for up to a week; **bone-in hams** (such as the rump or shank portions) will keep for up to two weeks. If you're baking a **raw ham**, it will only last 3 to 5 days after the sell-by date. If you are buying your ham well in advance of the date you intend to cook it, your best option would be to freeze it, making sure it is well-wrapped. An uncooked ham will keep for up to 6 months frozen, while a cooked ham will keep for only two months before the freezing begins to affect its flavor and quality.

Ham should never be thawed at room temperature on your kitchen counter-top. Place the ham covered on a dish in the refrigerator 2 days before baking to thaw.

Prepare the ham: Remove the packaging and place it fatty side up on a chopping board. Score the ham fat and skin(if any) on top with a sharp knife, making a diamond pattern about 1/4 to 1/2 an inch deep, with each parallel line about 1 1/2 inches apart. Don't cut into the meat itself, just into the layers of skin and fat. This allows any glazing to seep into the ham. Traditionally, a **clove** is inserted into the center of each diamond for flavor and decoration. *Remove the cloves before eating!*

Put the ham in a foil-lined roasting pan to make clean-up easier. Place the ham fat side up and leave uncovered. Some recommend adding half a cup of white wine or water to the base of the pan before baking, to prevent the ham from sticking.

Some recipes tell you to add enough water to come up 1 inch in the pan and cover the ham tightly with foil. This supposedly keeps the ham more moist as in the case with pre-sliced/spiral sliced hams which might get dry.

Glaze the ham: Regardless of what kind of glaze you use, separate a third of it and set the rest aside for later. Apply the glaze to the top of the ham with a pastry brush working it in between the scored lines. Keep the ham moist during cooking by brushing the meat with the reserved glaze at 20 minute intervals.

Keep a close eye on the color - if it starts to turn dark brown or black, make a "tent" with aluminum foil to cover the top of the ham while it finishes cooking.

Preheat the oven to 350°F for a conventional electric or gas oven. Set it to 325°F for a convection oven.

Place the ham in the preheated oven. The amount of cooking time will depend on the size off the ham and whether it has been pre-cooked or not. Follow the guidelines below for cooking times:

Bake a partially or fully-cooked preserved ham for 10 minutes per pound to reheat the ham completely through. **Bake a preserved ham that has not been precooked at all** for 20 minutes per pound. **Bake a fresh bone-in ham** for 20 to 25 minutes per pound or a **fresh boneless ham** for 30 to 35 minutes per pound.

Test the internal temperature of the ham. When a meat thermometer inserted into the center, but not touching bone, reads 160° F, the ham is done. If a ham has been fully pre-cooked, it is okay to remove the meat from the oven once it reaches a lower temperature of between 110° to 120°F, as you are simply reheating it for eating.

After you remove it from the oven baste the ham in its juices, cover and let it rest for at least 15 minutes before carving. This will allow the ham to finish cooking, while also letting the meat settle, making it easier to carve.

Make sure to save the bone which you can use to make a tasty bean soup. (Freeze it if not using within 2 days.)

GLAZES

The glaze you choose depends on your personal preferences - whether you like your ham sweet or herby and slightly spiced!

Mustard and brown sugar glaze: Mix equal amounts of honey mustard and brown sugar. 1/4 cup of each is a good measurement to go by, though this will vary depending on the size of the ham.

Brown sugar and maple syrup or honey glaze: Mix equal amounts of brown sugar and honey or maple syrup. Use about a 3/4 cup of each, depending on the size of the ham.

Honey thyme glaze: In a saucepan over a medium heat, combine 3 tablespoons of butter, 2 tablespoons of freshly chopped thyme, 1/4 cup of cider vinegar, 1/4 cup of honey, a tablespoon of brown sugar and a teaspoon of Worcestershire sauce. Stir constantly until the butter has melted and the sugar has dissolved, then remove from the heat.

GRILLED HAM & CHEESE SANDWICH

Butter one side of a piece of bread (white or rye) and place it in a cold skillet. Add a few slices of ham, then some slices of Swiss cheese, some mustard, a few more slices of ham. Top with another slice of bread buttered on one side which will be the top side. Turn the skillet to medium heat. When the bread is toasted on the bottom flip and toast the second side.

BEAN SOUP

1 (16 ounces) package of dried navy or Great Northern beans
7 cups water
ham bone or 2 ham hocks
1 cup chopped ham (optional)
1/2 cup each diced onion, carrot, celery
1 bay leaf
1/2 teaspoon salt and pepper

Put beans in a colander and rinse well under cold water. Discard any beans that look bad. Place beans, ham bone (ham hocks) and 7 cups water in large pot. Bring to a boil. Boil gently for 2 minutes, remove from heat, cover pot and let sit for 1 hour. Return to heat, add rest of ingredients. Simmer for 90 minutes to 2 hours - until beans are tender. Taste for salt. Add water if too thick. Remove ham bone or hocks, pull meat off bone and add back to the soup. Remove bay leaf.

Serve with a dash of vinegar and ketchup in the bowl.

Pork Chops Creole

Pork cooked in a slightly spicy red sauce until it becomes fork tender. Traditionally served with egg noodles.

Time: 2 hours
Servings: 2
Tools: large covered skillet
Serve with: egg noodles and a salad or green vegetable

INGREDIENTS:

2 **pork chops (bone-in)** or **pork steaks** or **4 small pork cutlets** 1/4" to 3/8" thick.

The idea is to fix 2 portions and freeze one for leftovers, so cook enough pork for 2 servings.

2 cups of **egg noodles** cooked

1/2 cup diced onion

1/2 cup diced celery

1/2 cup diced green bell pepper

Sauce:

1 cup (8 ounce can) **tomato sauce**

1 cup **ketchup**

1-1/2 cups **water**

2 teaspoons **worcestershire sauce**

3 tablespoon of **brown sugar**

1 teaspoon **Tabasco** or hot sauce

DIRECTIONS:

1. Mix the sauce ingredients in a bowl and set aside.

2. Heat a skillet large enough to hold the pork in a single layer to medium high heat with 2 tablespoons of oil. Brown the chops on both sides. Remove to a plate.

3. Reduce heat to low, add 1 tablespoon of oil to the pan if it is dry, add the onion, celery and green pepper and sauté until soft, about 5 minutes.

4. Add pork back to the pan. Pour the sauce over the chops. Bring to a boil and then reduce to a simmer. Cover the skillet and simmer on low for 1-1/2 to 2 hours. Stir every 15 minutes.

5. When done, remove the lid and continue to simmer until the sauce is thick. If it gets too thick before the end of the cooking time add some water. Taste for heat. If you like spicier add a few more drops of Tabasco sauce.

6. When the dish is almost done cook the egg noodles.

7. When done, remove chops to a plate. Put **half** of the sauce in a small bowl and leave the rest in the pan. Add cooked noodles to the hot pan and stir to coat with the sauce. If you want the noodles wetter add some of the reserved sauce. The sauce is potent so you may not want to overdo it.

8. Freeze half of the noodles with half of the pork for another meal.

For this recipe you may use: **pork tenderloin**, not pork loin which is an entirely different cut, **pork chops** or **pork loin cutlets**

If using a pork tenderloin: I have included directions for making a single serving or cooking a whole tenderloin if that is what you use. A whole tenderloin would be better if you are having company for dinner. If making a single serving using pork tenderloin open the pork tenderloin package. There should be 2 tenderloins. **Rinse** them under cold water, **pat them dry**. **Freeze** one of the whole tenderloins for another recipe like roast pork tenderloin. **Cut the other tenderloin** in 1/2 inch thick slices. **Set aside** 3 or 4 slices from the center of the loin for this recipe. Freeze the remaining slices. You can thaw them to make this recipe again or use in a stir-fry, make enchiladas or BBQ.

Time: 20 minutes for tenderloin slices, chops or cutlets. 1 hour for a whole tenderloin
Servings: 1
Tools: roasting pan or skillet
Serve with: buttered noodles or sweet potato, green vegetable

INGREDIENTS:	DIRECTIONS:
3 or 4 slices of **pork tenderloin** OR 1 or 2 **pork chops** OR 2 or 3 **pork loin cutlets** oil 1/4 stick (2 tablespoons)of **butter** or margarine 2 tablespoons **Grey Poupon mustard** 1/2 teaspoon **lemon juice** 1-1/2 tablespoons of **light brown sugar** (pack the sugar in the measuring spoon for correct amount)	1. Dredge the tenderloin slices, pork chops or cutlets in some flour seasoned with salt and pepper. 2. In a medium heat skillet with a few tablespoons of oil, fry the pork until done. A few minutes per side depending on thickness. 3. Remove to a plate. Add butter to the skillet on low heat and when melted, stir in the lemon juice and mustard. Stir and bring to a simmer for 2 to 3 minutes. Add the brown sugar and cook a few more minutes. Add chop/cutlet back to pan to reheat and serve.

USING A WHOLE TENDERLOIN:

Ingredients: 1/2 stick of **butter** or margarine,1/4 cup **Grey Poupon mustard**, 1 teaspoon **lemon juice**, 2-1/2 tablespoons of **light brown sugar** (pack the sugar in the measuring spoon for correct amount)

Directions: Set oven to 325°F. (You may grill it instead.) Place the tenderloin on middle oven rack in a shallow baking pan. Brush the tenderloin with oil and season all sides with salt and pepper. Bake for 45 minutes to 1 hour or until thermometer reads 140°F. Let it rest 10 minutes then slice on the diagonal in 1/2 inch slices. When pork loin is done make sauce as described above and have it ready to pour over tenderloin slices.

Pork Loin Roast

A pork loin roasts will provide a lot of meals. They usually come about 3 to 4 pounds and there is virtually no waste. **You may want to cut the roast in half** and freeze the unused portion for another time.

When you reheat any **leftovers** you will likely dry them out. I recommend leftovers be simmered in a vegetable or beef broth or a pork gravy mix for about 20 minutes. **Some other uses for leftovers:**

Chop it up and make some BBQ for sandwiches.
Chop it up and use to make enchiladas.
Slice it in thin strips and use for a pork stir-fry.

Time: 75 minutes
Servings: 4 for a half pork loin
Tools: roasting pan (and wire roasting rack if available)
Serve with: cooked apples, green vegetable, sweet potatoes

INGREDIENTS:

1, 3-4 pound **center-cut boneless pork loin cut in half.** (Freeze unused portion)

Double the seasoning amounts below if you roast the whole loin.

3 **garlic** cloves peeled and minced

1/2 tablespoon **salt**

1/2 tablespoon ground **sage**

1 teaspoon **rosemary**

1 teaspoon dried **thyme**

1/2 tablespoon black **pepper**

2 tablespoons **olive oil**

DIRECTIONS:

1. *30 minutes before you begin to roast set out the loin to come to room temperature.*

2. Preheat oven to 450°F.

3. In a small bowl combine all of the seasoning ingredients. Dry the loin with paper towels and rub the seasoning mix all over the loin.

4. Place the loin in a shallow roasting pan. (If you have a roasting rack place the loin on the rack in the pan.)

5. Roast for 15 minutes at 450°F. Then turn down the temperature to 300°F. Cook for another 30 to 40 minutes. Test the loin at 30 minutes for an internal temperature of 135°F. If not done continue to roast until it reaches that temperature. It will be a little pink and that is OK if it has reached 135°F. You don't want to overcook it or it becomes dry and tough. When done, remove, cover with foil and let rest for 10 minutes.

For this recipe you need a **pork** *tenderloin*, **not** *pork loin* which is an entirely different cut. Pork tenderloins usually come 2 in a package (though it is hard to tell there are two in there). For this recipe you may freeze the unused tenderloin and cook it another time.

You may see packages of pre-marinated pork tenderloins, I have never tried them. Pre-marinated packaged meat is often overly marinated. Pork tenderloin is a fairly delicate flavor so you can completely cover it up with too much marinade. You often see recipes for tenderloin that is marinated for a short time and that option is offered here.

GRILLING: prepare as below. May need less time on a grill. No need to sear the meat.

Time: 1 hour (2 - 3 hours if marinating)   **Serving:** 3 to 4 per tenderloin
Tools: roasting pan, large sauté pan.

INGREDIENTS:

1 package of **pork tenderloins** (Open the pork tenderloin package. There should be 2 tenderloins.) Rinse them under cold water, pat dry with paper towel and place on a large plate.

Freeze the second tenderloin or cook it as well, then cut it up in serving portions and freeze it. Reheat in beef broth.

You can marinade the pork which will add flavor or wrap the loin in bacon - see directions.

Marinade: *Double the amounts if cooking both tenderloins.*
Marinate for 1 to 6 hours in the refrigerator.

Place the loin(s) in a large zip-top baggie with: *(mix together)*

1/4 cup **soy sauce**,
1/8 cup vegetable or canola **oil**,
1 tablespoon of ground **pepper**,
2 teaspoons **minced garlic or garlic powder**
2 teaspoons **onion powder**
1 tablespoon **Dijon mustard**
OR use 1/2 cup of a bottled **Italian dressing.**

DIRECTIONS:

NOTE: Before cooking you will need to remove any "silver skin" on the loin. This is a thin patch of tough, shiny white skin often found on one side of tenderloins. Place the point of a sharp knife under the skin and saw back and forth while pulling at the skin.

1. Set oven to 400°F.

2. Heat a large skillet with a few tablespoons of oil to medium high heat. Pat the loin dry if you marinated it - if you don't it will not sear properly. Then place the loin in the skillet. Brown it on all sides. If you try to turn it and it resists leave it alone. When it has seared it will release from the pan.

3. Once seared place the tenderloin in a shallow baking pan and season with salt and pepper. (Omit salt if you used a soy sauce based marinade.) If you did not use a marinade you could use strips of bacon wrapped *around the tenderloin (like a candy-cane) secured with toothpicks - this will add moisture and flavor since tenderloins have so little fat.* Place the pan on the middle oven rack.

4. Roast for 35 minutes to 45 minutes or until a thermometer reads 135°F. Turn the tenderloin a few times during roasting. It may be a tad pink in the middle when done - that is OK.

5. After the cooked loin has rested for 10 minutes, slice tenderloin on the diagonal in 1/2 inch thick slices. Serve with some horseradish sauce (mayonnaise and prepared horseradish mixed together).

SMOKED SAUSAGE

Here are **2 recipes** for a meal with smoked sausage. The first is just some smoked sausage boiled and then broiled or browned in a skillet. The second is an easy one-pot meal. Smoked sausage, cabbage and potatoes all cooked together. The sausage will flavor the cabbage and potatoes.

Time: 30 minutes
Servings: 1
Tools: medium saucepan

INGREDIENTS:

1 serving **smoked sausage** cut into 2 pieces

DIRECTIONS:

Place the sausage in a small the pot and add enough water to just cover. Lightly boil it for 10 minutes (15 minutes if meat is frozen). This will make it very tender. Remove the sausage and then brown it on all sides in a skillet with a little oil or place it under the broiler for a few minutes on each side, but watch it closely if you use the broiler so it doesn't burn. You can also grill it.

Serve with mustard for the sausage or a mix of ketchup with a little horseradish. Serve with a side of Home Fries or Potato Wedges and a green vegetable or some BBQ beans or some boiled cabbage.

SMOKED SAUSAGE, CABBAGE AND POTATOES

INGREDIENTS:

1 serving **smoked sausage** cut into 2 pieces

a serving of **cabbage** cut in large pieces or chunks

1 large **potato**, peeled and cut into 8 pieces or 4 small red new potatoes or small Yukon Gold potatoes cut in half.

1 teaspoon **salt**

1/2 teaspoon **pepper**

DIRECTIONS:

1. Place everything in the pot and add enough water to just cover with water.

2. Bring to a boil, then reduce to a simmer, cover and cook for 20 to 30 minutes or until the cabbage and potatoes are just tender, not mushy. Remove the sausage, drain the water off the cabbage and potatoes leaving them in the pot and add a tablespoon or 2 of butter and toss.

NOTE: If you want a crispy sausage remove it after 15 minutes and place it on a broiler-safe pan. Put it under the broiler until one side browns, then turn it over until both sides are browned.

Serve with mustard for the sausage or a mix of ketchup with a little horseradish.

Good for breakfast, lunch, brunch or even dinner with a nice salad. The combinations of what you put into a quiche are endless. This is an "all-purpose" recipe. It's a great way to use leftover vegetables.

Prep & Cooking Time: 1 hour
Serving: 4 - 6
Tools: skillet, pie plate, 2 mixing bowls, baking sheet, whisk

INGREDIENTS:

1, 9 inch, frozen unbaked deep-dish **pie shell** - the kind that come in an aluminum pie pan. They come 2 to a package. Freeze unused shell.

The Custard:

3 large **eggs**

1-1/2 cup **milk** (or 1 cup milk and 1/2 cup cream)

1 teaspoon **salt**

1/2 teaspoon ground **pepper**

Filling Ingredients:

1 to 2 cups of a mix of **filling** ingredients like mushrooms, bacon, onions, bell pepper, asparagus, frozen chopped spinach, peas, ham, etc.

The Cheese:

1 to 2 cups **grated cheese** - Cheddar, Swiss, Gruyere, etc.

DIRECTIONS:

1. **Cook your filling ingredients.** They must be cooked through and fairly dry if not previously cooked.
   Frozen spinach must be thawed and squeezed dry, *raw spinach* must be cooked down in a skillet until all water is removed.
   Mushrooms must be sautéed in a little butter until brown.
   Frozen peas need to be boiled or microwaved a few minutes and drained.
   Asparagus needs to be steamed until just tender.
   Onions, bell pepper need to be sautéed until just tender.
   Bacon needs to be fried, drained and crumbled.

2. Sprinkle half of the cheese over the bottom of the pie crust.

3. Whisk together the eggs, milk (or cream), salt, pepper until frothy. Pour into the pie crust.

4. Top with the remaining cheese.

5. Place pie crust shell on a baking sheet.

6. Bake on the middle rack in a 350°F oven for 35 to 40 minutes - until it is golden brown and the eggs have set. (Give it a jiggle and if it moves a lot, let it cook 5 more minutes. If it barely jiggles it is ready. It should still be a little jiggly in the center when you take it out of the oven.)

FILLING OPTIONS: (to the basic custard above you add the following and bake according to above directions.)
Quiche Lorraine: 8 slices chopped bacon, 1 diced yellow onion, 1 cup gruyere cheese
Mushroom Quiche: 16 ounces crimini mushrooms sliced thinly, 1/2 diced yellow onion, 2 minced garlic cloves, 2 cups swiss or gruyere cheese
Ham and Asparagus Quiche: 1/2 diced yellow onion, 1/2 pound chopped asparagus, 1 cup diced ham or chopped deli ham, 2 cups swiss or cheddar cheese

SAUSAGE & CHEESE QUICHE

Good for breakfast, lunch, brunch or even dinner with a nice salad.

Prep & Cooking Time: 1 hour
Serving: 6
Tools: skillet, 2 mixing bowls, baking sheet, whisk

INGREDIENTS:

- 1, 9 inch, frozen unbaked **deep-dish pie shell** - the kind that come in an aluminum pie pan. They come 2 to a package. Freeze unused shell.

- 2 large **eggs**

- 1 cup **evaporated milk**

- 3/4 teaspoon **salt**

- 1/2 teaspoon ground **pepper**

- 1 pound of **pork sausage** - you can buy ground in a package like hamburger or your favorite sausage that comes in a tube (like Jimmy Dean, etc)

- 1/2 cup thinly sliced **onion**

- 1/3 cup chopped green **bell pepper**

- 1-1/2 cups shredded **sharp Cheddar cheese**

- 1 tablespoon chopped fresh **parsley**

- 1 tablespoon **all-purpose flour**

DIRECTIONS:

1. Brown the sausage in a skillet and break it up. Remove to paper towel to drain. Pour off all but 1 tablespoon of fat from the skillet.

2. Sauté the onion and bell pepper in the skillet just until tender - about 3 minutes.

3. Put sausage, onion, peppers, cheese, flour in a bowl and mix.

4. Place piecrust shell on a baking sheet and spoon the mixture into the shell making an even layer.

5. In a bowl whisk together the eggs, milk, salt, pepper and parsley until smooth. Pour over mixture in shell.

6. Bake on the middle rack in a 350°F oven for 35 to 40 minutes - until it is golden brown and the eggs have set. (Give it a jiggle and if it moves a lot, let it cook 5 more minutes. If it barely jiggles it is ready. It should still be a little jiggly in the center when you take it out of the oven.)

SALADS

A salad can be a side dish or a main course depending on what you do with it. By adding vegetables like broccoli, cauliflower or asparagus that have been steamed to tender and then chilled in an ice bath, or cold beets, or fruit like strawberries, pears, oranges or sliced grilled or pan-fried chicken or strips of deli turkey and/or ham you make a salad a nice, lighter meal. Nuts like almonds, pecans or walnuts add crunch as well as beneficial nutrients and fiber. If making it the main course I like to use at least some spinach for the added nutrients. Use whatever additions you like besides the usual carrots, celery, red onion, bell peppers, cucumbers, tomatoes and radishes.

TYPES OF LETTUCE / SALAD GREENS

On these pages you will see a description of different kinds of salad greens and suggestions for how to use them. Always wash your greens as there may be some residual sand and dirt even though they are bagged. Keep them stored in a bag or container. Leafy green lettuces sometimes get a bit flaccid after a few days in the fridge. Pop them in a bowl of cold water, cover and refrigerate for several hours then drain well. It will "wake them up."

Iceberg, also known as crisphead. It has a round, compact pale-green head and will last for over a week in the refrigerator because it is 96% water. Generally the mildest of the lettuces, iceberg let-  tuce is valued more for its crunchy texture than for its flavor or nutritional value of which there is little compared to other greens. *Never cut iceberg with a metal knife* as that speeds up the browning of the edges where cut. It's best to pull it apart or use a plastic knife.

Romaine or cos lettuce. The heads consist of long pale-green leaves that are crisp in texture. When preparing romaine, it is best to discard the dark outer leaves as well as the darker tops of the inner leaves. The crispest, most flavorful parts of the romaine are the lighter leaves near the cen-  ter. You will sometimes see these packaged as **romaine hearts**. It is the traditional lettuce used in **Caesar salad**.
A good dose of vitamin A and K.

Red leaf lettuce is similar to romaine lettuce, except it has red-tinged leaves. Lettuce is most often eaten raw in salads, but it can also be braised, steamed, sautéed and even grilled to create a different addition to an entree or side dish. Choose closely bunched, fresh-looking leaves. Avoid brown, wilting edges. Rinse and dry romaine lettuce thor-  oughly on paper towels. Refrigerate in plastic bag for use within 1 week.
Just 4 calories per cup, with nearly half of the daily recommended dose of vitamins A and K and a good source of manganese.

Butterhead – There are 2 main varieties of butterhead lettuce. The first is **Boston** or butter lettuce and the second is **Bibb** or Kentucky limestone. Butterhead lettuces have small, round, loosely formed heads with soft, buttery-textured leaves rang-  ing from pale green on the outer leaves to progressively smaller pale yellow-green on the inner leaves. The flavor is sweet and succulent. Because the leaves are quite tender, they require gentle washing and handling. Both varieties lend themselves to lighter dressings because of their soft texture and mild flavor.

Arugula – also called rocket or rucola. When young, the dark green leaves are small and tender, but as they mature they become large and a bit tough. Arugula is a member of the mustard family but it is not as bitter as mustard greens. Its  taste is peppery and a little nutty. The best dressings for arugula are citrus-based or those enhanced with sweeter vinegars like balsamic.

Belgian endive - also called French endive, witloof, witloof chicory, Belgium chicory. The unique oval shape, soft satiny texture, and slight bitterness all mean endive's a great addition to any salad.  It's scoop-like shape and firmness makes the perfect "spoon" for appetizers.

Radicchio. Pronounced "rah-dick-ee-yo." You usually find this deep-red-purple vegetable sold as a compact round head. The bright coloring makes it stand out. Radicchio is bitter and nutty in flavor. It can be eaten raw, mixed with other greens or cooked. When cooked, the red-purple hue  turns brown and what was once bitter be-comes sweet. It is often sliced in half, doused with a little extra-virgin olive oil, salt and pepper and grilled as a side dish.

Spinach – a perennial favorite; the leaves are bright green. It comes in large bunched leaves with stems and needs to be well rinsed as it tends to be very sandy. It can also be purchased

pre-washed in bags. **Baby spinach** leaves are smaller and more tender. Avoid purchasing spinach leaves that are starting to yellow. Spinach takes to a variety of dressings as it is neutral and mild. Because of its high nutritional value it's good to mix some with  other less nutritional greens or just an entire salad made with the baby spinach variety.
High in vitamins A and K.

Kale is being called "the new beef," "the queen of greens" and "a nutritional powerhouse." Until recently kale was mostly a cooked green, but now it is showing up everywhere raw in salads. High in fiber, more iron than beef, lots of  vitamin C and super high in vitamins A and K. Also touted to be high in antioxidants, an anti-inflammatory and good for your cardiovascular system because it can lower cholesterol!

Spring Mix - also called Mesclun, is a mix of assorted small, young salad leaves. Spring mix is

made up of any of 16 different greens and lettuces of varying tastes and textures, including red romaine, baby spinach, radicchio, green romaine, red oak leaf, mizuna, red leaf, lollo rosso, arugula, red mustard, green mustard, red chard, frisee, and tatsoi. About half of the greens and lettuces are sweet and mild while others provide a complementary slightly bitter edge. It is usually sold in a plastic bag or container and is sometimes available loose in a bin so you can bag as much as you want or need and pay by the pound. It will last 5 to 7 days in your refrigerator.

Spinach Salad

This is a classic salad with lots of nutritional value. It's a salad that is more like a vegetable. You could add some thinly sliced grilled chicken and make this a meal. Amounts are given for 1 serving.

Salad greens: raw spinach or raw baby spinach. (Remove stems if using regular spinach, but if using baby spinach you can leave the stems on as they are not tough, but tender.)

Wash greens under cold water and spin dry. Put greens on a salad plate or in a salad bowl. Top with:

2 or 3 **mushrooms:** Rub only the mushrooms you will use under cold water to remove any dirt. *You may have heard you never run mushrooms under water because they will absorb it. However, I have seen tests that disprove this.* Do not clean all the mushrooms as they keep longer if you do not wash them. Remove the mushroom stems - grab the stem and give it a twist/tug.) Slice thinly.

Some thinly sliced **red onion**

crumbled fried **bacon**

Some **pecans or walnuts**

(optional) Some **pickled beets**

Croutons

Additional options: chopped hard-boiled egg, some sliced avocado, thinly sliced red bell pepper, salad tomatoes, carrot...

DRESSINGS: a hearty dressing works best because the spinach has a lot of flavor. Blue cheese, balsamic vinaigrette or warm bacon dressing work well. (See recipes.)

Caesar Salad

Anchovies give this dressing its unique flavor. If you do not like anchovies - there is really no substitute. (I am not fond of them, but have no problem with them in this salad.) And don't bother making this dressing without it. It is just not the same. This dressing is very specific if you want to make it the classic way. You will also want a **wedge of parmesan**, not the pre-grated kind. There is **no need to add salt** - the anchovies and parmesan have plenty.

INGREDIENTS:

a serving of **romaine** lettuce - use leaves from **romaine hearts** torn into pieces.

1 or 2 **anchovy filets** packed in oil or a teaspoon of anchovy paste found in a tube

1 large clove **garlic** peeled

1/2 teaspoon **lemon juice**

1 **egg yolk** (raw)

1/4 teaspoon Dijon mustard

2 tablespoons **extra-virgin olive oil**

1/8 cup **vegetable or canola oil**

1 tablespoon **grated parmesan cheese**

a handful of **croutons** - you will find varieties just for Caesar salad at the market

DIRECTIONS:

1. Chop the anchovy and garlic. Then, using the flat side of a knife blade, mash them into a paste. (You could also put them in a garlic press.) Place in a medium glass bowl.

2. Add the egg yolk to the bowl and whisk until smooth. Add lemon juice and mustard - whisk to mix.

3. In a very thin stream, almost drop by drop, whisk in the olive oil then the other oil whisking constantly until thick and glossy.

4. Whisk in the grated parmesan.

5. Place your romaine on top of the dressing mixture in the bowl. Toss with 2 spoons or tongs to mix well.

6. Transfer salad to a plate and top with croutons and some shaved parmesan cheese. (Use a vegetable peeler to shave the parmesan from the wedge.)

Greens and Fruit Salad

This is a nice change from a typical tossed salad.

Salad greens: use romaine, green or red leaf lettuce, Spring Mix or baby spinach.

Fruit: Peel an **orange** or **tangerine** and cut it in thin slices across the membrane, not with the membrane. Cut the slices in half-moons. (Figure 1 orange or tangerine a person.) Or use fresh strawberries, peaches or pears that have been sliced.

Dressing: raspberry vinaigrette or balsamic vinaigrette (See *Vinaigrette Dressings*)

Options: add a few of the additions below.

> **pecans** or **walnuts** or **sliced almonds**
>
> thinly sliced **red onion**
>
> **crumbled bacon (especially if you use pears)**
>
> **crumbled blue cheese or goat cheese**
>
> finely sliced **carrot and/or radish**

Wilted Lettuce

This is a classic Southern salad that uses the Warm Bacon Salad Dressing.

INGREDIENTS:

Use **spinach, baby spinach** or **leaf lettuce.** (Remove stems from spinach, unless it's baby spinach, whose stems are not tough, but tender.) **Do not use iceberg lettuce** because of its high water content - turns the lettuce to mush.

crumbled bacon

some thinly sliced **red onion**

thinly sliced **mushrooms,**

pecans or **walnuts**

(optional)1 **hard-boiled egg** sliced or chopped

DIRECTIONS:

Place all of your ingredients in a salad bowl. Pour in the warm bacon dressing and toss well.

BLUE CHEESE DRESSING

Use this dressing on the following:

A Salad Wedge. Popular in the 50's and 60's this salad has made a comeback. Cut a wedge of iceberg lettuce. (Cut the head in half from the crown to the root and then each half in half from the crown to the root. Place on a plate. *Possible additions: cherry or grape tomatoes, some crumbled bacon, French's Fried Onions.*

Spinach Salad: Baby spinach is preferred, but any spinach will do. Wash it, spin it dry. *Possible additions: some crumbled bacon, some pecans or walnuts, sliced raw mushrooms, thinly sliced red onion, sliced beets (from a can), French's Fried Onions.*

Belgian Endive: Pull the small head apart, rinse and spin dry. Fan the leaves out on a plate and drizzle a little dressing on each "spoon." *Possible additions: some chopped tomato, finely chopped bell pepper, finely chopped pecans or walnuts.*

Spring Mix, romaine, bibb or leaf lettuce salad: Spread some dressing in the bottom of your bowl and put all your ingredients on top. It's easier to mix the greens and the dressing this way rather than putting it on top. Stir up from the bottom to coat the lettuce. *Possible additions: cherry or grape tomatoes, bell pepper, carrot, red onion, grated cheddar cheese, sliced radishes, cucumber slices, French's Fried Onions.*

Time: 10 minutes to prep, at least 2 hours to meld flavors
Servings: 4
Tools: mixing bowl

INGREDIENTS:	DIRECTIONS:
4 ounces good **blue cheese crumbled.** (Maytag, Stilton are expensive, **gorgonzola**, an Italian blue, is quite good, but cheaper.) 3/4 cup **mayonnaise** 3/4 cup **sour cream** 1/4 teaspoon **pepper** 1/8 teaspoon **salt** 1/4 teaspoon lemon **juice** 2 tablespoons **milk**	1. Place 1/2 of the crumbled blue cheese in a small bowl. 2. Add 1 heaping tablespoon of the mayo and with a fork, mash the blue cheese into the mayo. 3. Add the rest of the cheese, mayo, the sour cream, pepper and the lemon juice. Mix well. 4. Ideally it should sit in the fridge several hours before use so the flavors have a chance to really meld together. If you want it a bit thinner add 1 tablespoon of milk at a time until the consistency you prefer. ***This will keep about 5 days in the fridge.***

WARM BACON SALAD DRESSING

This dressing is easy to make especially if you have fried some bacon to put on a salad like a spinach salad. It's also the dressing you use with a wilted greens salad. **It does not work well on iceberg lettuce** because of its high water content - turns the lettuce to mush. Use spinach, baby spinach or leaf lettuce. (Remove stems from spinach, unless it's baby spinach, whose stems are not tough, but tender.)

Time: 15 minutes
Servings: 1
Tools: frying pan, mixing bowl

INGREDIENTS:

1 slice of thick-cut **bacon** or 2 slices thin-cut bacon

2 tablespoons red wine **vinegar**, apple cider vinegar or balsamic vinegar

1 teaspoon sugar or 2 teaspoons **honey**

1/2 teaspoon Dijon or brown **mustard**

1/2 teaspoon ground **pepper**

DIRECTIONS:

1. Fry the bacon and remove to a paper towel to drain. When cooled, crumble into pieces, but not too fine. **Do not discard the bacon fat** - leave it in the skillet.

2. Add the vinegar, mustard, sugar and pepper to the bacon fat on medium heat. Mix well and scrape the bottom of the pan. When the mixture begins to steam it is done.

3. Pour the warm dressing over your salad greens and toppings and toss. Top with crumbled bacon.

Vinaigrette Dressings

A vinaigrette is a simple dressing of oil and vinegar and the most typical for a salad. This recipe makes enough for several salads - just refrigerate what you do not use. It keeps almost forever because of the vinegar. Making your own ensures that you are not getting a bunch of additional chemicals and salt you find in typical bottled varieties.

There are several **types of vinegar** and each gives the dressing a different flavor. The most common are **white, apple cider, red wine** and **balsamic**. While **vegetable or canola oil** are acceptable oils for a vinaigrette, **extra-virgin olive oil** is much healthier and has more flavor.

Raspberry vinaigrette is a popular dressing, but you will need to make the vinegar yourself unless you can find it at a market – buy a bag of frozen **raspberries**, place them in a container and add 1 cup **white vinegar** and 1/2 tablespoon of **sugar**. Let it sit for a couple of days in the fridge. Then **strain** the raspberries and press them in the strainer to remove all the liquid from them. Discard the raspberry mash. **Taste** the vinegar. If it is still too bitter add a little more sugar and taste. Repeat as necessary so it is no longer bitter, but not sweet. Raspberry vinaigrettes go especially well with salads that have slices of citrus like oranges or fruit like pears. (SEE Greens and Fruit Salad recipe.)

Lemon vinaigrette has become popular and requires no mixing. Just before you are ready to eat your salad sprinkle a little **extra-virgin olive oil** over your greens and then squeeze some fresh lemon juice on top.

When you make a vinaigrette you are making an **emulsion**. Vinegar and oil do not want to mix, they want to separate. An emulsion helps them to blend. In the recipe below you will use a vinegar of your choice. Sometimes it's good to mix a cider or red wine vinegar with some balsamic vinegar as balsamic is very flavorful vinegar. Use two-thirds white, apple or red wine to one-third balsamic. **There is a "golden" ratio for any vinaigrette - 3 parts oil to 1 part vinegar.** But you should always taste your dressing to see if it needs more of one or the other as different oils and vinegars may change the rule. **Do not refrigerate the mixture for at least 30 minutes.**

There are **3 ways to make the emulsion** – in a bowl using a whisk, a blender or in a jar. If you use the whisk method you will have to whisk in the oil in a very thin slow stream while constantly whisking.

INGREDIENTS FOR A BASIC VINAIGRETTE:

1/4 cup vinegar
3/4 cup oil
1 teaspoon **mustard** - Dijon, brown, grain (avoid yellow) **OR mayonnaise OR honey.** (These
    are stabilizers that help emulsify the mixture.)
1/2 teaspoon salt and pepper

Whisk method: Put the vinegar and mustard in a **glass or steel** (never aluminum) bowl. Whisk until smooth. Now **slowly, almost by drips,** drizzle in the oil while whisking vigorously until all the oil is used. *TIP: put a kitchen towel under your bowl to keep it from moving while you whisk.*

Blender or jar method: Place all of the ingredients in a blender or a jar. Blend for 30 seconds on high or shake for 1 minute vigorously.

It's always better to put your vinaigrette dressing in the bottom of your bowl, add your salad mixture and toss the lettuce bringing the dressing up from the bottom. Pouring dressing over the top can over saturate your lettuce and make it heavy or even a bit wilted.

ITALIAN VINAIGRETTE:

1/4 cup **red wine vinegar** (or 1/8 cup red wine and 1/8 cup balsamic)
3/4 cup **extra virgin olive oil** or other oil
1 teaspoon **mustard** - Dijon, brown, grain (avoid yellow) **OR mayonnaise OR honey.** (These
    are stabilizers that help emulsify the mixture.)
1/2 teaspoon **salt and pepper**
Add herbs like oregano, basil, thyme and garlic (a few cloves grated on a microplane or 1 teaspoon
    of garlic powder) which will give it an "Italian" dressing flavor. If you do this the dressing should
    sit for several hours so the herbs have a chance to flavor the mixture.

HONEY DIJON VINAIGRETTE:

3/4 cup **oil** of your choice
1/4 cup **vinegar** - white, apple cider, red wine
1 tablespoon Dijon **mustard**
1 tablespoon **honey**
salt and pepper to taste.

BALSAMIC VINAIGRETTE:

3/4 cup **extra virgin olive oil** or other oil
2 tablespoons **balsamic vinegar**
2 tablespoons **red wine vinegar**
1/4 teaspoon **Dijon mustard**
1 teaspoon **minced fresh herbs** (e.g. parsley, chives, tarragon)
Kosher salt and ground white pepper (or freshly ground black pepper), to taste

RASPBERRY VINAIGRETTE:

3/4 cup canola **oil**
1/4 cup **raspberry vinegar**
1 teaspoon honey
salt and pepper to taste.

FISH

Fresh Fish:
Fresh fish should never have a strong fishy odor. Obviously, if you put it close to your nose there will be a slight scent of the sea. When you get it home rinse it under cold running water, pat dry and wrap loosely in wax paper. Keep it in the coldest part of the refrigerator. Use it within 2 days. If you are not going to cook it within 2 days you must freeze it. Some suggest freezing fish by placing it in a container and covering it with milk. When thawed it preserves the flavor.

There are basically two types of fish – the light and flaky kind like cod, haddock, pollock, tilapia and the meatier kind like salmon, tuna and swordfish. All may be cooked in several ways, but the meatier ones are more grill-friendly as they tend not to fall apart on a grill rack. Swordfish and tuna are among the highest in mercury so you shouldn't eat them too often.

Frozen Fish:
Much fish today comes flash-frozen. Even some of the "fresh" fish in a grocery display was frozen and thawed. Always ask if "fresh" fish was previously frozen. Once thawed it deteriorates rapidly. No matter how many paper towels you use to absorb the water in the fish it will retain water. From my experience, thawed frozen fish does not do well with a coating when pan-frying. The water in the fish turns the coating to mush and it does not adhere well.

Thawing Frozen Fish:
Typically, frozen fish is thawed in the refrigerator and that may take overnight. A quicker method is to place the pouch of frozen fish in a bowl filled with cold tap water and keep it refrigerated. It will thaw much faster. When you are ready to cook the fish, cut a slit in the pouch and drain out any water that has come out of the fish. Then place the fish between paper towels. Frozen fish often retains a lot of unwanted water from the freezing process. Some suggest thawing fish in cold milk.

The Recipes:
These recipes work with any fish. The only difference is the time it takes to cook it. Obviously, a thicker fish like cod takes longer than a thin filet of tilapia. These days, many people like thicker fish like tuna or swordfish a bit pink in the middle. That is up to you when cooking it. I have devoted a separate section to salmon because of its popularity and the many ways you can cook it and enhance it with marinades, glazes and sauces.

Dredging:
It is common to dredge fish for sautéing or pan-frying in a skillet with some type of coating. It is not necessary to coat the fish, but it does impart a little more flavor and texture. It also protects the outer layer of fish from drying out and sticking to the pan.

The simplest form is to **dredge** the filet in some flour or cornmeal or a mix of the two or the now very popular panko crumbs. Shake off the excess, salt and pepper it and let it sit a few minutes so the coating adheres. This will add a browned and crispy texture to the fish. You will add some oil to your pan for frying rather than brushing oil directly on the fish before cooking.

Marinades:
A simple marinade is a great way to add flavor to fish and it does not take long to impart the flavor - no more than 30 minutes. The meatier fish like

salmon, tuna, and swordfish take marinades especially well. Marinade should be patted off the surface before cooking – a dry fish cooks best.

Try a little soy sauce, lemon or lime juice, some garlic or ginger. **If you marinate for too long** and you have used any kind of citrus, the acids will actually begin to break down the fish and turn it mushy when cooked.

PAN FRYING

Cooking fish in a skillet browns the outer flesh of the fish. This imparts flavor as the natural sugars and fats caramelize.

- Fish should not be cold. Let it sit out for at least 15 minutes before cooking.

- Pat the fish dry. That's important to getting a good browning.

- Brush both sides of the fish with a little bit of cooking oil – canola or olive – avoid butter as it cannot withstand a high cooking temperature. Salt and pepper both sides.

- Preheat your skillet on medium-high heat.

TIP: to test if your pan is hot enough, put a few drops of water in the pan. If it sizzles and steams away in a few seconds you are good to go. If it pops and steams away instantly it's a little too hot. If it sits there – it's not hot enough.

- Place fish in pan (skin side down if it has skin). Turn down heat to medium if cooking a thick fish as you don't want it to burn before it is half-way cooked. If skin curls, gently press the corners of the filet so the skin makes contact with the pan.

- Once you place the fish in the pan leave it alone for 2 - 3 minutes (5 to 6 minutes for thick fillets). Do not try and turn the fillet until it has a chance to sear. Cook the second side for 1 to 2 minutes more or 4 to 5 minutes for thicker fish.

Only turn the fish once. Don't turn it back and forth.
- When the flesh just begins to turn opaque on

top gently turn the fish and cook a few more minutes.

Thickness of your fish will obviously determine how long it takes to be cooked through. A thin fish will only take a manner of a few minutes on each side. If the top of the fish begins to change color that is a sign it is time turn the filet. If the fillet is thick you can look at the sides of the filet and see how far up it is turning white on the bottom. If you are unsure how done it is just stick a fork in it and pull back the flesh and look into the fillet.

BROILING

Broiling is a good way to cook a lot of filets if you are feeding a crowd, but works fine for a single serving as well. Normally broiled fish is not coated in any type of crumbs as they will burn.

- Fish should not be cold. Let it sit out for at least 15 minutes before cooking.

- Pat the fish dry. That's important to getting a good browning.

- Brush both sides of the fish with a little bit of cooking oil – canola or plain olive – avoid butter as it cannot withstand a high cooking temperature. Salt and pepper both sides.

- Preheat your broiler.

- Place the over rack so the fish will be 4 to 6 inches from the broiler element.

- Thin fish (less than 1/2 inch) will not have to be turned, but thicker fish should be turned half way through. You will have to watch the fish to know when it is done or when it needs turning.

Figure 10 minutes of cooking time per inch of thickness or fraction thereof.

Always keep a watchful eye on fish under a broiler or you may burn it. One minute can make the difference between done and burned.

You can turn off the broiler when the fish is about 2 minutes from being done. The burners will stay hot for a while and continue to cook the fish.

BAKING/ROASTING

Roasting concentrates the flavor. You can also season the fish with any spices or herbs of your choice.

- Fish should not be cold. Let it sit out for at least 15 minutes before cooking.

- Pat the fish dry. That's important to getting a good browning.

- Brush both sides of the fish with a little bit of cooking oil – canola or plain olive – avoid butter as it cannot withstand a high cooking temperature. Salt and pepper both sides. You can also dredge it in some cornmeal or breadcrumbs with this method.

- Place the over rack in middle of the oven

- Preheat your oven to 400°F.

- Place fish on a baking sheet or in a shallow pan.

Figure 15 to 20 minutes of cooking time per inch of thickness, but check it after 15 minutes.

A thin layer of lemon rings on top of the fish is a nice addition to this method of cooking.

POACHING

Small fish or fillets are poached by simmering in a small amount of seasoned liquid in a skillet. The liquid can be strained when done and used in making a sauce. Poached fish is not coated with anything like breadcrumbs.

It is important not to let the liquid boil - only barely simmer. This keeps it from overcooking too quickly.

A typical poaching liquid might be some white wine and chicken or vegetable broth with some sliced onion, some lemon slices and salt and pepper. Put enough liquid in a skillet - enough to just reach the top of the fish once it is put in the pan. Bring the liquid and seasoning to a simmer, add fish and simmer on low heat until fish is cooked. If you wish, remove fish, strain the liquid, put it back into the skillet and reduce on high heat until you have about an 1/8 cup. Turn off heat. Add a little butter, lemon juice and parsley, swirl until melted and pour over fish.

GRILLING

Grilling works especially well with thicker fish like tuna, salmon and swordfish. Because of its steak-like texture it holds up well to a grill without falling apart. Be sure to grease the grill rack well. Flaky fish tends to come apart on a grill so purchase a fish basket that is made for grilling on place it on some non-stick foil on the grill. Be sure to grease the basket. Pat the fish dry and brush with canola or olive oil.

SAUCES, HERBS AND SUCH FOR FISH

The following are some ideas for how to "dress" your fish for serving...

Citrus:
Fresh lemon or lime is always the perfect accompaniment to fish.

Tartar Sauce
The classic fish condiment. (1 serving)
Mix together:
- 1/3 cup mayonnaise
- 2 tablespoons minced sweet or dill pickle (Use the small pickles. If you use large ones or spears, remove the pith and seeds. You can use relish, but press it in a small sieve to remove water.)
- 1/2 tablespoon minced shallot or onion
- 1 teaspoon lemon juice
- 2 tablespoons finely chopped fresh parsley
- 1 tablespoon rinsed capers (if you have them).

Lemon Pepper:
Use lemon pepper seasoning instead of plain pepper when preparing your fish.

Lemon Sauce:
When fillets are done pan-frying you can make a quick lemon sauce in the pan which will be a nice addition. Remove the filets to a warm plate,

squeeze about 2 tablespoons of lemon juice into the pan. Add 4 tablespoons of white wine, dry vermouth or even vodka. Let it simmer for a minute to burn out the alcohol. Turn off the heat and mix in a tablespoon of butter. Sprinkle with some fresh parsley. Pour sauce over the fish.

Salsa:
A canned salsa with a little added lime juice is also a tasty topping for fish. Warm it up and spread it over the cooked fish or place it on the filets when baking.

Peppers:
Chop up some bell peppers (any color) and onion; cook until tender and spread over the fish.

Honey:
A good "topping" for baked salmon is a little honey and lemon juice.

SALMON

Salmon has become extremely popular these days. It is a very versatile fish and can be prepared in many ways. No matter how you cook it, at most it will take about 20 minutes to cook it. If you overcook salmon it becomes very dry.

Atlantic salmon are a farmed salmon. The fish are fed a diet that can be full of growth hormones and coloring agents to turn the flesh pink. *The Environmental Defense Fund suggests consuming no more than one meal per month consisting of Atlantic salmon.* Some salmon is now farmed on the west coast.

Wild caught salmon is the best to buy. All Alaskan salmon is wild caught. Avoid farmed salmon if possible.

King or chinook salmon has a high fat content and buttery texture and is high in those good omega- 3s.

Coho salmon are found from British Columbia to Alaska. They are a mild but flavorful fish.

Sockeye salmon are a smaller variety of salmon that is also high in omega-3s. It has a stronger flavor and does especially well on a grill. You can also find it canned. If available it's your best bet, though more expensive.

Pink salmon is most often used for canning.

The most common **cuts of salmon** you find are **salmon steaks** and **salmon filets**. Steaks are cross-cut across the salmon and retain the skin and central bone while filets are cut from the side. You are more likely to find **small pin bones** in a steak than a filet. Rub your fingers across a filet and feel for any pin bones. Pull them out. You generally will not be able to find pin bones this way in a steak.

If you are not experienced with cooking salmon you should always test it about half way through the cooking time so you get an idea of how long it will take to finish cooking. Simply take a fork and pull back the flesh in the thickest part. If the center looks a bit raw you are not done. Salmon is done when it is the same color throughout and flakes easily with a fork.

Broiling, baking and **grilling** are the most common ways salmon is cooked. **Poached** and **steamed** salmon are other options which keep the salmon very moist.

BROILING AND BAKING

If broiling, place your salmon filet on a piece of foil on a broiler safe pan. It will go on an oven rack that is about 6 to 8 inches from the broiler element. If you find the top is burning before the filet is done, just turn off the broiler, close the door and let the residual heat in the oven finish cooking it.

If baking, place your salmon filet on an oven safe dish or pan on the middle rack of an oven heated to 400°F. It will take 10 to 25 minutes depending on the thickness of the filet. When baking you can brush with some butter and add chopped fresh dill, salt and pepper or put some lemon slices or top or a quick topping is can of tomatoes and green chiles (like *Rotel*) drained and spread over the filet.

POACHING

Place your salmon in a small skillet. You will need a poaching liquid. It can be water, chicken or vegetable broth or a broth you make by boiling some herbs and vegetables like celery and carrot and onion. You can also add white wine, lemon or lime juice to the poaching liquid. Salt and pepper should be added as well. The liquid should just come to near the top of the filet, but not cover it. Gently simmer the filet until done.

A **cucumber sauce** is a classic topping for poached salmon — this is enough for 1 filet: 1/4 cup chopped cucumber (peel and seed it first), 2 tablespoons of sour cream or greek yogurt, a dash of salt and pepper, a teaspoon of dill and 1/2 teaspoon vinegar.

STEAMING

You can use a steamer to cook the filet on the stovetop or create a bag with foil and bake it in the oven.

If using a steamer you can add herbs and spices to the water or use a broth. You can also put lemon slices on top of the filet or a mixture of finely chopped tomato, onion and bell peppers that you will eat with the fish.

If steaming in a foil bag in the oven, you can put some lemon slices on top with a little melted butter or a mixture of herbs and spices or a mixture of finely chopped tomato, onion and bell peppers that you will eat with the fish. Seal the bag so no steam escapes.

GRILLING

Salmon, like tuna and swordfish, takes well to the grill. Of course, it is still somewhat delicate and can stick to the grill. A fish grill basket is helpful or you can put it on a piece of foil. If you are looking for grill marks, then be sure to oil your grill rack well and brush oil on the filet.

MARINADES

Salmon can be enhanced with a marinade. You don't need to marinade long - 30 minutes is plenty. If you use citrus in your marinade just be careful as it will cook the fish if left in the marinade too long. Soy sauce and teriyaki sauce are a good, simple marinade. A few tablespoons is plenty. Just turn the filet once while in the marinade.

GLAZES AND SAUCES

Soy and Brown Sugar Glaze:
- Mix together: 1/4 cup brown sugar and 2 tablespoon soy sauce.
- Brush the top of the filet with oil and sprinkle with salt and pepper.
- Place under the broiler for 6 to 8 minutes depending on thickness of the filet. In the last 2 minutes brush with the glaze mixture. When done, brush with more glaze.

Maple Syrup Glaze
- Mix together 1/4 cup maple syrup and 1 tablespoon Dijon mustard in a saucepan over medium heat. Simmer until slightly thickened.
- Remove from heat and brush on the salmon
- Brush more glaze on salmon halfway through broiling.

Dijon Dill Sauce
- In a small saucepan heat 1 tablespoon of oil and 1 tablespoon of butter until it melts.
- Add 1 tablespoon of finely chopped shallot or onion and sauté until soft.
- Add 1/2 cup dry white wine and cook until liquid is reduced by half.
- Reduce heat and whisk in 1 teaspoon Dijon mustard, 1/2 tablespoon dried dill (or 1 tablespoon fresh dill chopped), 1/4 teaspoon salt and pepper.
- Remove from heat and whisk in 1 tablespoon of cold butter. Pour over cooked salmon

Horseradish Cream Sauce
- In a small saucepan mix 1/4 cup sour cream, 2 teaspoons of prepared horseradish, 1 teaspoon black pepper. Warm the mixture until the sour cream melts. Pour over cooked salmon.

ORANGE SALMON

This recipe can be done in the microwave or roasted in the oven.
Salmon takes to sweet well.

Time: 15 to 25 minutes
Servings: 1
Tools: small microwave safe baking dish or
a small oven safe baking dish (pie pan or cake will work)
Serve with: twice-baked potato or fried rice, Brussels sprouts

INGREDIENTS:

1 **salmon filet** patted dry

1 tablespoons of melted **butter**

3 tablespoons **orange juice**

1 teaspoon **cornstarch**

salt and pepper

DIRECTIONS:

Microwave Method:

1. Place the filet in the baking dish.

2. Mix together the melted butter, orange juice, salt and pepper and cornstarch. Pour over the salmon.

3. Cover with plastic wrap leaving one corner vented. Microwave on high for 3 to 6 minutes. Check half way through with a fork. If your microwave doesn't rotate, rotate the dish. It's done when it flakes easily with a fork. Let it rest for a few minutes. Pour source over fish when serving.

Oven Method:

1. Same as Steps 1 and 2 above.

2. Bake at 400°F for15 minutes. Check for doneness and cook more if necessary. Let rest for a few minutes and pour sauce over to serve.

SALMON CROQUETTES

These croquettes are moist and creamy. Use a good canned salmon, like **Red Sockeye** if you can find it. I am going to give you 2 recipes. The first is the best. The thick roux makes the croquettes so moist and creamy, but requires chilling the mixture several hours. But if you are in a hurry you can use the quick version at the bottom.

Time: 15 minute prep/3 hours refrigerate / 10 minutes to cook
Servings: 1 (makes 2 large croquettes)
Tools: medium sauce pot, small baking dish or small skillet
Serve with: cole slaw, pickled beets, egg noodles with butter and parsley or rice pilaf

INGREDIENTS:

1 small tin (7-1/2 ounces) of **salmon** – Red Sockeye or Pink

1 tablespoon **prepared horseradish**

3 tablespoons **breadcrumbs or cracker crumbs**

1/2 cup **cornflake crumbs or cracker crumbs** for breading

2 tablespoons of **oil and butter** for frying

White Sauce:

1-1/2 tablespoons **butter**
2 tablespoons **flour**
1/2 cup **warmed milk**
salt and pepper

DIRECTIONS:

1. **Make the white sauce:** melt 1-1/2 tablespoons of butter in a small saucepan and then stir in the flour. Cook for 2 minutes on medium heat, stirring constantly.

2. Add a little milk at a time, stirring constantly until any lumps disappear and the mixture becomes VERY thick like a heavy paste. (This is a thick roux.) Remove from heat. Discard half of the thick mixture.

3. Add flaked salmon, horseradish and breadcrumbs to the thick roux. Mix well. Spread in a shallow pan (like a pie plate), refrigerate for 30 minutes uncovered, then at least another 90 minutes covered.

4. When the salmon is well chilled and you are ready to cook, divide the mixture in half and form 2 patties about 3/4 inch thick. Place them on a plate.

5. Sprinkle each patty with cornflake crumbs and lightly pat them onto the patty. Turn and do the same to the other side. If you are not going to fry them right away, refrigerate them, otherwise they will tend to "melt" in the frying pan.

6. Add oil and butter to a skillet on medium high heat. When the pan is hot add the patties and fry on both sides until golden brown, 3-4 minutes per side.

Drizzle with lemon to serve.

QUICK RECIPE:

Omit the roux/white sauce, instead add one beaten egg, use 1/3 cup bread or cracker crumbs, 2 tablespoons finely minced onion, 1 tablespoon finely minced green or red bell pepper, 1/2 tablespoon prepared horseradish. Mix all of the above with flaked salmon. Refrigerate 30 minutes then proceed with Step 4 above. (You can also bake these in a 400 degree oven for 25-30 minutes, turning once.)

SHRIMP

My favorite shellfish is shrimp. It's a very versatile fish and can be used in so many dishes, but my favorite way to eat shrimp is steamed in their shell. Shrimp have the least amount of mercury of any fish — another good reason to eat them!

Most shrimp we find these days come frozen in bags unless you live on a coast where they are fished and you can find them fresh. Like much fish today what you see unfrozen at a fish counter in your grocery store may have been previously frozen. If fresh shrimp (without heads) in the shell are available to you I recommend them. They will be more flavorful and tender.

Preparing shrimp usually involves removing the head (if it has one), the shell and "sand vein." The tail can be left on especially if you are streaming them to eat by themselves or grilling them. Leaving the tail on gives you something to hold onto as you eat the shrimp. I like to remove the tail if I am adding them to a dish. Packaged shrimp will say if the shrimp have been shelled and deveined. Shrimp in a shell will always need to be deveined.

To de-shell a shrimp, the tail is held while gently removing the shell around the body. The tail can be detached completely at this point, or left attached for presentation purposes.

Shrimp have a "sand vein" — a euphemism for their digestive tract! Removing this is called deveining." The sand vein can be removed by making a shallow cut lengthwise down the outer curve of the shrimp's body, allowing the dark ribbon-like digestive tract to be removed with a pointed utensil or your finger. Special deveining tools are available but a small knife or even toothpicks can be used. Alternatively, if the tail has been detached, the vein can be pinched at the head end and pulled out completely with the fingers. On large shrimp there is a "blood vein" along the inner curve of the shrimp's body. This is removed as well. Once the shrimp has been shelled and deveined rinse them under cold water. *Removing the vein is not essential — it is not poisonous, but could be a little gritty and is mostly tasteless.*

Shrimp are usually boiled, steamed, pan-sautéed, roasted or grilled. The biggest problem with shrimp is that they cook quickly and **if you overcook them they become tough and rubbery.** When they begin to curl they are done.

Many of the frozen shrimp available may even say they are cooked, but I find them to be a bit underdone and rubbery. I have gone to parties where they put out a shrimp ring they bought at their local market. I can't eat them. They are underdone and chewy. I went to school in Maryland so I know my shrimp and how they should be.

Buying: When you buy a pound of shrimp in a bag or even if they are loose in a counter they are marked by size and count like: small 51/60, meaning there are 51 to 60 shrimp per pound. Medium will be 41-50, medium-large is 36-40 and large is 31-35. One thing to remember is that when you cook shrimp they shrink in size almost by half. Medium to large is your best bet if you are eating them by themselves; mediums and medium-large are good if you are adding them to a stir fry, rice dish or pasta dish.

㉚ MARYLAND-STYLE STEAMED SHRIMP

Though this recipe is called Steamed Shrimp, they are actually boiled. (That's what they call it in Maryland!) Anywhere I have served these shrimp people go crazy for them. Steamed shrimp are often served as an appetizer, but you can make a meal of them, too.

I have to give two versions of this recipe: one for shrimp in their shell (the original recipe) and one if you use a frozen shrimp that has been shelled and deveined (that somewhat mimics the true recipe).

This recipe will work with any amount of shrimp, but at least a half of a pound or more works best.

VERSION ONE:
You will use shrimp in the shell, with or without heads. If they were frozen, thaw them first.

In a saucepan that will hold all the shrimp put a layer of the shrimp, salt them well and sprinkle them with 1 tablespoon of **Old Bay Seafood Seasoning**. (No substitutes!) l. Make another layer, add salt and Old Bay. Repeat until all shrimp have been layered.

Now add equal parts of water and white or cider vinegar just to the top of the shrimp — yes, that's a lot of vinegar, but you won't even know it was in there, trust me. They are in a shell so it takes a lot of salt and vinegar to season them.

Cover and bring to a simmer. Depending on the size of the raw shrimp it will take 3 to 5 minutes. When they have curled remove them from the heat and drain immediately. Pour onto a plate and let them cool. They will continue to cook a bit in their shell.

Eat them slightly warm or chill them for an hour.

VERSION TWO:
This is my recipe for "steamed" shrimp when you do not have fresh shrimp. You will use frozen shrimp that have been peeled and deveined or even shrimp from one of those shrimp rings. **First, thaw the shrimp if frozen.** You can put them in a bowl of tap water to speed up the thawing.

You are going to toss the shrimp into a pot of boiling water, so choose a pot that will hold enough water to cover the shrimp when you add them.

Boil the water, remove it from the heat and toss in the shrimp. Let them sit in the hot water for 2 to 3 minutes. Depends on the size of your shrimp. When they turn pink or curl drain the pot, but leave the shrimp in it.

Add the following **per 1/2 pound** of shrimp:
1 tablespoon cider vinegar
2 tablespoons *Old Bay Seafood Seasoning*
Toss the shrimp until they are coated.
Remove to a plate and them them cool. Eat them at room temperature or chill them.

Shrimp Sauce: (for dipping)
Mix together:
1/2 cup ketchup
1 tablespoon prepared horseradish or more if you like it hotter
(optional - a few drops of lemon juice)

You don't find many recipes so simple and easy and quick as Shrimp Scampi. You can **add pasta** — linguine, spaghetti, penne or even egg noodles to this recipe or just make the shrimp and **serve over rice**.

You may use **fresh or frozen shrimp**. Shrimp in their shells have to be shelled and deveined. Thaw frozen shrimp in some tap water. It will only take a about 10 minutes.

Time: 15 minutes
Servings: 1
Tools: large skillet
Serve with: rice or pasta and a green vegetable

INGREDIENTS:

1 serving of **shrimp** - however many you like

NOTE: You can leave the tail shell on or pull it off before cooking. Cooking the shrimp with the shells on will impart a little more flavor. Shelling the shrimp before cooking them will make the shrimp a lot easier to eat.

2 tablespoon **butter** (unsalted preferred)

2 tablespoon **olive oil**

salt

1/2 tablespoon **minced garlic**

1/2 teaspoon **red pepper flakes**

1 teaspoon ground black **pepper**

1 tablespoon **chopped parsley**

1 tablespoon **lemon juice**

1 teaspoon **lemon zest**

1 serving of pasta or rice

DIRECTIONS:

If adding a pasta, you can start cooking it before you start cooking the shrimp so it is ready when the shrimp are done.

1. Heat a sauté pan to medium-high, add the olive oil and butter. Once the butter melts add the garlic and red pepper flakes. If using unsalted butter, sprinkle with salt. Sauté for a minute, or until the edges of some of the garlic begins to brown. Don't burn the garlic!

2. Now spread the shrimp in an even layer in the pan and sauté on medium heat for about 5 minutes turning a few times. Shrimp are done when they have just curled. Don't overcook them or they become tough. (*Add drained warm pasta when shrimp are done and toss it into the mix. Let it cook for 1 minute or just serve over come cooked white rice.*)

3. Remove from the heat, add the parsley, lemon juice, zest and black pepper and mix well.

SHRIMP CREOLE

A classic New Orleans dish that is quick to make. Make it as spicy as you like.

Time: 20 minutes
Servings: 2
Tools: large skillet or large pot
Serve with: a salad

INGREDIENTS:

1/4 stick **butter**

1/2 cup **onion** chopped chicklet size

1/2 cup **celery** chopped chicklet size

3/4 cup chopped chicklet size **green bell pepper**

20 **shrimp** - (36-40 count-bite size). **Tails removed.** (You can use fresh or frozen. Thaw frozen shrimp before cooking.)

1/2 tablespoon chopped **garlic**

1/4 cup **green onions** chopped (green stems and onion parts)

1/8 cup chopped **fresh parsley**

1, 28 ounce can **diced tomatoes** drained (save the juice)

1/2 teaspoon **Cayenne**

Dash of **Worcestershire Sauce** (and I do mean a mere dash!)

1/2 teaspoon of **hot sauce** - like Tabasco. (Use more if you like it spicier.)

1 tablespoon **Old Bay seafood seasoning**

salt to taste

2 cups cooked **white rice**

DIRECTIONS:

1. Toss shrimp with Old Bay in a bowl to coat. Set aside.

2. In a large skillet or pot melt butter. Add onions, celery. Season with salt and cayenne. Sauté mixture until onions and celery just start to become soft - about 3-4 minutes. (If you cook them too long they will get too soft and you'll lose texture.)

3. Add tomatoes, green pepper and garlic, dash of Worcestershire and hot sauce. Raise the heat to high then reduce to simmer for another 5 minutes. If mixture get's too dry add some of the juice from the drained tomatoes. You do not want it to be too juicy like a soup just very moist!

4. Now taste it for salt, cayenne and hot sauce levels. Add more if needed.

5. Add shrimp, 1/2 of the green onions and 1/2 of the parsley and simmer until shrimp are done (when they have curled and are no longer translucent.) Takes about 3 to 5 minutes. Raw shrimp will take a bit longer. If mixture seems too dry add a little more of the tomato juice.

Serve over rice. Sprinkle top of each serving with some green onions and fresh parsley.

MARYLAND-STYLE CRAB CAKES

This is the classic recipe for crab cakes. Now, you **MUST** use real crabmeat, not that imitation stuff. If you can find blue-fin crab that is ideal.

Marylanders often eat their crabcakes with crackers and sliced tomatoes on the side. You can make 4 large crabcakes, instead of 8 small ones, and eat them on a bun with a little lettuce and tartar sauce (recipe, page 102) and a slice of tomato like a burger.

Time: 1-1/2 hours
(most of this time is to allow the crab cakes to set-up before cooking)
Servings: 4 - you should make 8 cakes with this recipe
Tools: large skillet. mixing bowl
Serve with: cole slaw, macaroni and cheese, pickled beets

INGREDIENTS:

1 pound **blue-fin crabmeat** - lump or backfin

2 slices of **dry white bread**, no crust, made into breadcrumbs in blender.

1 teaspoon **parsley flakes or fresh parsley**

salt and pepper to taste

1/4 teaspoon **dry mustard**

1 teaspoon **Old Bay Seafood Seasoning**

1 scant teaspoon **worcestershire sauce**

1 well-beaten **egg**

2 generous tablespoons **mayonnaise**

DIRECTIONS:

1. In a medium mixing bowl, gently, with a fork, fold crabmeat, breadcrumbs, parsley, salt and pepper, dry mustard together. Gently - you do not want to break up the crabmeat.

2. Add worcestershire and beaten egg, mix again gently.

3. Add mayo and gently mix.

4. Make 8 crab cakes. Place on a plate, cover with plastic wrap and refrigerate for at least 1 hour.

5. Heat 1/4" of oil in a skillet and fry on both sides in a medium-high heat skillet until brown. About 3 to 4 minutes per side. Remove to paper towel and drain briefly.

6. Eat leftovers in a day or two or freeze leftover cakes.

COLE SLAW

Here are 2 recipes for a cole slaw - a vinegar slaw and a mayonnaise based creamy slaw. Adding crumbled **blue cheese** to either of these recipes makes a tasty addition. Don't buy bags of pre-shredded slaw mix, use fresh cabbage. Since you cannot buy a small amount of cabbage (well, you can, just ask the produce guy to cut one in half for you) you can boil the unused cabbage for a supper side dish with some smoked sausage.

Time: 20 minutes
Servings: 2
Tools: large mixing bowl, mandolin slicer

INGREDIENTS:

1 small head of **green cabbage** or a half of a large head. You will use **2 cups thinly sliced cabbage** (or substitute 1 cup with red cabbage)

1/4 cup shredded **carrot**

2 tablespoons finely chopped red or yellow **onion**

1/4 cup chopped **green bell pepper**

1 tablespoon **celery seed**

1 tablespoon **cider vinegar**

1/2 tablespoon **sugar**

1/2 cup **mayonnaise**

1 teaspoon **salt and pepper**

DIRECTIONS:

1. Cut the cabbage in half. Remove the hard core. Cut each half in half. You can either shred it (slice it thinly) or use a mandolin to slice it. Place 2 cups in a large mixing bowl.

2. Add all of the other ingredients. Mix well. Taste it. Too sour? Add a little more sugar and mix. Too sweet - add a little more vinegar and mix.

3. Refrigerate at least 3 hours, several is better so the flavors can blend.

VINEGAR (SWEET & SOUR) COLE SLAW

INGREDIENTS: Same as Creamy Cole Slaw **but omit the mayonnaise and use 1/4 cup cider vinegar and 1 tablespoon sugar.**

DIRECTIONS: Same as Creamy Cole Slaw. Taste it for sour/sweet balance.

Cucumber Salad

This is a mayonnaise-based cucumber **side dish**, but is also delicious as a **cucumber salad dressing** on leaf lettuce or Spring Mix. Amounts are based on a large cucumber about 9 inches long or an English cucumber which are called "seedless" though they have seeds which are very small. English cucumbers are more expensive. Adjust your amounts if smaller.

*TIP: Peeling a cucumber – some people do not like cucumber because they tend to burp it later on. I have found that if you **peel it and remove the seeds** (even small ones) there is none or little of that cucumber belch. For this recipe after you peel it, cut it in 3 lengths. Use a vegetable peeler or a small spoon to dig out the seeds. Slice it as thin as you can or use a mandolin slicer.*

Time: 15 minutes to prepare, chill for at least 3 hours
Servings: 4
Tools: medium glass mixing bowl

INGREDIENTS:

1 **large cucumber** peeled and seeded, sliced thinly as possible, then cut slices in half.

1 small **onion** peeled and sliced thin. Cut slices in half.

NOTE: If you are making this primarily as a salad dressing chop the cucumber and onion smaller.

1 tablespoon **celery seed**

2 teaspoons **apple cider vinegar**

2 teaspoon sugar

1/2 cup **mayonnaise**

1/2 teaspoon **salt**

1 teaspoon ground **pepper**

DIRECTIONS:

1. Place all of the ingredients in a bowl. Mix well. Taste the liquid. It should not be too tart or too sweet. You want to taste the vinegar, but it should be balanced with the sugar. Adjust vinegar or sugar as needed.

2. Refrigerate for several hours to let the flavors meld. It will be much juicier after it sits because the cucumbers will give up their water and that is what you want.

Herbed Potato Salad

A good alternative to a mayonnaise-based potato salad is one made with a kind of vinaigrette. You can eat it warm, at room temperature or cold. Like many recipes this one is fluid — you can add whatever you fancy to your taste.

Time: 30 minute prep
Servings: 2
Tools: 4 quart pot, medium mixing bowl

INGREDIENTS:

10 small red **new potatoes** or small Yukon Gold potatoes. (If you use the large versions, use 3 or 4 potatoes.)

2 tablespoons **cider or red wine vinegar**

6 tablespoons **oil** (corn or extra-virgin olive)

1 teaspoon Dijon or spicy **mustard**

1 teaspoon **salt and pepper**

1 tablespoon fresh chopped **parsley**

2 tablespoons finely chopped **green onion**

1 teaspoon chopped **dill** or dry

You may add any or all of the following:

1 teaspoon chopped **chives**

1/2 teaspoon **thyme**

1/2 teaspoon **rosemary**

DIRECTIONS:

1. Scrub the potatoes under cold water. Boil the potatoes until they are tender. Insert a knife to test. There should be no resistance. Remove and let cool. If you don't like potato skins in your salad you will peel them when they become cool enough to handle.

2. Meanwhile, in a small mixing bowl add the vinegar and mustard. Whisk together. Slowly drizzle in the oil while whisking constantly until all the oil is incorporated.

3. Add all the other ingredients and mix. Let sit until the potatoes are ready.

4. When the potatoes are cool enough to handle, slice the small potatoes in half or if you used larger potatoes cut them in sixths or eights depending on their size. You want large bite size pieces. Put them in a bowl and pour the mixture over them. Toss well. Taste for salt as potatoes take a lot.

You can serve it warm when finished or chill it for several hours. If chilled, bring to room temperature first for better flavor.

Potato Salad

Recipes for potato salad abound. Every Mom has her own version. I have never had the same one twice. There are mayonnaise based and mustard based and vinegar based varieties. This is a general mayonnaise based recipe. If you like a **mustard potato salad** just reduce the mayo a little and add a tablespoon of mustard. *Potato salad will last only 3 days in the fridge.*

Time: 1 hour prep, 4 or more hours to chill
Servings: 2
Tools: pot for boiling potatoes, mixing bowl

INGREDIENTS:

3 large **red potatoes**

1/4 cup finely **chopped celery**

1/8 cup finely **chopped carrot**

1 tablespoon finely **chopped onion**

1/4 cup finely **chopped green bell pepper**

1 tablespoon **celery seed**

1 tablespoon **apple cider vinegar**

mayonnaise (or some people prefer *Miracle Whip*)

salt and **pepper**

paprika

(optional) 1 or 2 hard **boiled eggs** chopped or sliced in quarters to place on top or to add to the mix

DIRECTIONS:

1. Put the whole potatoes in a large pot and cover them with salted water. Boil uncovered until potatoes are tender all the way through – 20 to 30 minutes. (Test with a knife.)

2. Remove the potatoes and let them cool until you can handle them - 10 to 15 minutes.

3. Meanwhile, add the celery, carrots, onions, green pepper and celery seed (and chopped eggs if you use them) to a medium-size mixing bowl.

4. When the potatoes are cool enough to handle, but still warm, peel the potatoes (or leave the skins on). To peel – drag the blade of a knife across the potato. Slice the potatoes in 1/2 inch rounds and place them in the mixing bowl.

5. Add the vinegar, a little salt and pepper, and gently toss. Now add 3 heaping tablespoons of mayonnaise, toss gently and mix well. If the mixture looks too dry add a little more mayonnaise. You will want it to be moist – the potatoes will absorb some of the mayo as it chills in the fridge. Give it a taste – can you taste the vinegar? It should be subtle, but it should be there. Need more salt?

6. Let the mixture sit on the counter for about 15 minutes to cool. Sprinkle top with a little paprika. Cover and place in the fridge to chill for several hours. **NOTE: leave the cover slightly off the bowl for the first hour so any steam from the warm potatoes can escape otherwise that will make your salad watery.**

FRIED RICE

Perk up some plain white rice with this recipe. You begin with **cold rice** — either some leftover rice or rice you cook ahead of time and refrigerate for a few hours. You can add leftover chicken or shrimp to make it a complete meal. Fried rice is a good side with fish, pork chops, pork tenderloin and baked chicken. *TIP: if cooking your rice in advance use chicken broth instead of water to give the rice more flavor.*

Time: 20 minutes
Tools: a large skillet

INGREDIENTS:

As mentioned above, fried rice **works best with cold rice** - leftovers or some rice you cook in advance and refrigerate for at least a few hours. Fresh cooked rice will tend to get mushy if used for frying. You want to use a medium or long-grain - and not that stuff that takes 5 minutes. Boil-in-Bag rice works well as will any medium or long-grain rice you have prepared.

NOTE: since this recipe is based on some leftover rice or an amount you previously cooked no amounts are given. You can make this a chicken fried rice or shrimp fried rice by adding some leftover chicken or shrimp shredded or cut into bit size pieces.

You can add whatever you want to a fried rice, but whatever you add you want it to be **cut, sliced or chopped small** so it cooks quickly. Consider using some of the following: carrot, celery, onion, mushrooms, thawed frozen peas, spring onion, asparagus, broccoli, snow pea pods. For a cup of cooked rice you want to add about 1/3 cup of any mixture of the above. Use 1/2 cup of diced up leftover chicken or shrimp if adding that.

You will need some **soy sauce**.

(optional) **scramble an egg** in a bowl and have it ready. *If you do not add egg, omit Step 3 below.*

DIRECTIONS:

1. For each cup of rice add 2 tablespoons of oil and 1 tablespoon of butter to a skillet on **medium high heat**.

2. When the pan is hot add the vegetables and stir-fry for about 3 minutes. *(If adding thin asparagus or pea pods, wait and add it in Step 4.)*

3. Move them all to one side, pour the egg into the clear space, roll it around to spread it in a thin layer. When it has cooked chop it up with your spatula.

4. Now add your rice (asparagus, pea pods and any previously cooked chicken or shrimp). Mix thoroughly and give the mixture a good toss and mix around the skillet about every 15 seconds. Do this for about 5 to 7 minutes.

5. Just before serving add 1 tablespoon of **soy sauce**. Mix thoroughly. Fry another minute while constantly tossing. Serve.

RICE PILAF

Rice Pilaf makes plain white rice something much more tasty and it only takes a few extra, simple steps. A pilaf is rice usually cooked with a broth rather than water and often contains some herbs, vegetables or nuts. You can freeze leftovers to make a fried rice another day.

Time: 30 minutes
Tools: medium saucepan with a lid

INGREDIENTS:

This recipe is based on using 1 cup of **long-grain white rice. Read the package** to determine the amount of water (in this case, broth) you need for 1 cup of rice. You can also use a wild rice like Bob's Red Mill, but wild rice takes much longer to cook. You can use brown rice, but brown rice by its nature tends to be sticky.

Typically **chicken broth** is used, but you could use a canned vegetable broth.

A: Use one or more of the following for the pilaf, but keep it simple — 2 or 3 at most.
1/4 cup diced onion or green onion or leeks
1/4 cup diced celery
1/4 cup thinly sliced carrot
1/4 cup diced mushrooms
1/4 cup peas
1/4 cup or pine nuts
1/2 teaspoon fresh chopped thyme

B: One or more of the following can will be added at the very end:
1 tablespoon fresh chopped parsley
1/8 cup sliced almonds
thinly sliced green onion
chopped chives

DIRECTIONS:

1. Add enough oil or butter to cover the bottom of the saucepan and bring it to medium-high heat. Add items from "A" and sauté until translucent - about 3 minutes.

2. Add the rice, mix to coat with the oil or butter and cook for about 3 minutes stirring often.

3. **Add the broth** (preferably pre-heated in a measuring cup). Mix. Bring to a **boil, cover** the pot and **reduce to a simmer.** Cook for the amount of time as directed on the package of rice. Do not remove the lid at any time. When done remove the pot from the heat. **Do not remove the lid** and do not stir it until it has rested for at least 5 minutes.

4. After it has rested add items from "B" and fluff them into the rice with a fork.

Pasta Salads

Here are 2 recipes for pasta salads. The first is your typical mayonnaise-based macaroni salad and the second a traditional vinaigrette-based pasta salad. You can put them together quickly, they just need a few hours to refrigerate.

Time: 30 minutes to make / 3 or more hours to chill well (or see note to shorten time)
Servings: 2
Tools: medium mixing bow, pot for boiling pasta

MACARONI SALAD

INGREDIENTS:

1-1/2 cups **macaroni** (or mini-penne or ziti)

1/4 cup finely chopped **celery**

1/4 cup finely chopped **carrot**

1 tablespoon finely chopped onion

2 hard-boiled **eggs** chopped

3/4 cup or more **mayonnaise**

1 teaspoon each **salt and pepper**

DIRECTIONS:

1. Boil macaroni according to package instructions. Drain, rinse with a little cold tap water, drain well and put in a medium mixing bowl.

2. Add celery, carrot, onion, egg to bowl and mix.

3. Add mayonnaise, salt and pepper and mix well. Taste for salt. If it seems too dry add a little more mayo. *After it chills the macaroni will absorb a lot of the mayo so it should be good and moist before you chill it.*

4. Place uncovered in the refrigerator for 30 minutes, then cover tightly.

NOTE: If you are in a hurry, you can put the dish in the freezer uncovered for 20 minutes. Stir it after 10 minutes. Remove and stir again. Cover and put in the fridge for another hour.

PASTA SALAD

If you are making a pasta salad go with a different shaped pasta like ziti, corkscrew, farfale, mini penne, etc., Tri-color pasta (red, green, yellow) is typical for a pasta salad. You will basically make a simple Italian vinaigrette for the pasta — see the recipe in *Vinaigrette Dressings* or use a bottled Italian dressing that you like. Boil 1-1/2 cups pasta according to package directions.

Use whatever **vegetables and herbs** you like — carrot, onion, spring onion, bell peppers, zucchini, cherry tomatoes cut in half, broccoli or asparagus you have blanched (steamed until just tender and put in a cold water bath to stop the cooking and lock in the color), fresh chopped parsley, oregano, basil, chopped chives.

Toss the **pasta** and **vegetables** with some **vinaigrette**, about 1/4 cup, plus 1/3 cup **grated parmesan cheese** and chill for at least a few hours. Taste for salt.

CREAM OF BROCCOLI OR CAULIFLOWER SOUP

Broccoli and cauliflower are interchangeable in many recipes. When I say broccoli here I mean cauliflower as well. This recipe will make 2 to 3 servings. Freeze leftovers in serving-size containers. This recipe explains a **plain broccoli soup** and a **broccoli-cheese soup**. This is a chunky style soup. If you like it completely smooth you will have to put it into a blender. See *Using a Blender* below. A hearty soup and a salad or a sandwich makes a great winter supper.

Time: 30 minutes
Servings: 2
Tools: medium or large saucepan

INGREDIENTS:

2 tablespoons **flour**

1 cup or more **milk or see NOTE**

3 cups of **broccoli** cut up cut into 2 inch pieces. It does not have to be chopped fine. Split any thick branches.

1/4 teaspoon grated **nutmeg**

salt and pepper to taste

(option-for a broccoli-cheese soup) some american or cheddar or Velveeta cheese - about 1/2 cup grated cheddar or 6 slices of american or 1 inch slice from the block of Velveeta.

DIRECTIONS:

1. Put about 1/4 inch water in the saucepan. Add 1/2 teaspoon salt. Add broccoli, cover, bring to a boil, then reduce heat to a simmer so it steams for 5 minutes. Drain off water. Mash the cooked broccoli with a potato masher or fork leaving it as chunky as you like it.

2. Sprinkle 2 tablespoons flour over the broccoli and stir in. Cook for about 2 minutes on medium heat stirring often to cook out the flour taste.

3. Add 1 cup of milk. Stir. Add more milk if it is too thick - it should not be too thin or too thick. (Add optional cheese.) Bring to a simmer and let cook uncovered for 15 minutes stirring often. Taste - add more cheese if you like cheesier. Taste for salt and pepper. If it gets too thick while simmering add more milk.

NOTE: To make a richer (and higher calorie version) use 1/2 cup chicken broth or milk and 1/2 cup cream (OR half-and-half) to replace the milk. You might do this for a special occasion or if cooking for guests. Add more broth if it gets too thick.

USING A BLENDER: If you prefer a smooth soup after you add the milk, but before you add any cheese, put the mixture in a blender. **Hold your hand on the blender lid.** Pulse it a few times first. If you start with puree it can blow the lid off. Pulse then puree until smooth. Pour back into pot, add cheese if you want, and simmer for 15 minutes.

CONFESSION: Sometimes I use a can of cream of broccoli soup to make this, but not if using cauliflower. Most people have no idea I did it. By the time it's done it looks and tastes like it was all from scratch! I cook the broccoli, mash it, **omit the flour**, add the canned soup, milk and cheese and cook for about 15 minutes.

LEEK AND POTATO SOUP

This is one of my favorite soups. A hearty soup that eats like a meal. You may see recipes for a "loaded" leek and potato soup which usually means bacon and cheese are added like a loaded baked potato. Options are given below to do that. You may omit the bacon/ham if you want it vegetarian.

NOTE: Cleaning leeks... leeks can get a lot of sand between the layers. You will use all of the leek up to the joint where it splits into leaves. Trim off the root end. Cut the leek lengthwise down the middle from the joint to the root end. Turn it and make another slice so you now have 4 quarters. Now slice the leek in 1/4 inch rings. Place the leeks in a sieve or colander and run cold water over them tossing them with your hands to mix them around and make sure they are getting well cleaned. Set aside and let drain.

Time: 45 minutes
Servings: 3 - 4
Tools: large pot — 4-6 quart

INGREDIENTS:

4 tablespoons **butter** or margarine

3 **leeks** cleaned and chopped (*see note above*)

3 slices of diced **bacon OR** 1/2 cup of finely diced ham

1 stalk of **celery** diced

4 large **potatoes** peeled and diced in 1/2 inch cubes (6 cups of diced potatoes). Yukon Gold potatoes make it extra good.

1, 14 ounce can of **low-sodium chicken broth**

2 cups **milk OR** 1 cup milk and 1 cup half and half

salt and **pepper** to taste

DIRECTIONS:

1. In a large pot of salted water, boil the diced potatoes for 5 minutes. Drain the pot and put potatoes in a bowl. Rinse out the pot and return it to the stove.

2. Sauté ham (or bacon) in the pot until it is browned. (If using bacon remove all but 2 tablespoons of the bacon grease when done.)

3. Add butter, celery and leeks to ham/bacon and sauté until soft and translucent. Stir often. Sauté until the mixture is dry and there is no liquid — about 10-15 minutes.

4. Add all but 1/2 cup of the potatoes back to the pot. Add the broth, milk, salt and pepper. Mash the remaining potatoes with a fork then add to the pot. Simmer the soup until potatoes are tender — about 5-10 minutes. Taste for salt.

5. Add more milk if too thick. Soup should be a little thick.

If you want to make this a "loaded" leek and potato soup, after you place it in the bowl add some grated cheddar on top with a dash of sour cream and some chives.

LENTIL SOUP

A hearty soup that is good for you - fiber and protein.

Time: 2 hours
Servings: 4 - 6
Tools: 6 to 8 quart pot or Dutch Oven

INGREDIENTS:

1, 16 ounce bag of dried *Lentils du Puy* (small, dark greenish lentils) **WASHED AND RINSED SEVERAL TIMES** in a strainer or colander. Pick out any lentils that look "bad."

10 cups **water**

3 slices **diced bacon or a ham hock**

1 cup finely chopped **onion**

1/2 cup finely chopped **celery**

1/2 cup finely chopped **carrot**

1 large clove **garlic** minced

1/2 teaspoon, crushed **oregano**

1, 14 ounce can **diced tomatoes**

2 tablespoons **red wine vinegar**

2 teaspoons each **salt** and **pepper**

(**optional**) finely chopped **spinach** or **kale** - about 1/2 cup.

DIRECTIONS:

If you use a ham hock, simmer it covered in 4 cups of water for 90 minutes before you begin cooking the soup.

1. Place the washed lentils in a large glass bowl. Boil 4 cups of water and pour it over the lentils. Add 2 tablespoons of salt. Stir. Cover with plastic wrap and set aside for 1 hour, then drain.

2. When the lentils are done soaking, in a large 6 to 8 quart pot, render the diced bacon until almost crispy unless you are using a ham hock in which case go to Step 3. Discard all but 2 tablespoons of bacon grease.

3. Add celery, carrot and onion to pot with bacon fat and sauté until just soft - 4 to 5 minutes. (If using a ham hock and not bacon, add 2 tablespoons of butter for sautéing the celery and onion.)

4. Add drained lentils, garlic, oregano, vinegar, tomatoes with juice, salt, pepper and 10 cups water. (If using a ham hock, use the water it was boiled in as part of the water you add and add the hock to the pot.) Cover and simmer for 30 minutes. Taste a lentil for doneness. If not tender cook until they are done. Stir occasionally. If at anytime the soup seems too thick add more water.

5. (Remove ham hock when done.)

SERVING:
Stir in about 1/2 teaspoon red wine vinegar when you put the soup in the bowl.

Sandwich Spreads

A few recipes for making some basic sandwich spreads — perfect for lunch or dinner with some soup or a salad or a snack on crackers.

PIMENTO CHEESE

INGREDIENTS:
8 ounce block of **sharp cheddar or white Vermont cheddar** *(avoid pre-shredded bags of cheese)*
3 tablespoons **chopped green olives**
1, 4 ounce jar **diced pimentos** *well-drained (put into a small fine-mesh strainer and press to remove water)*
1/4 cup **chopped pecans**
2 or 3 **heaping** tablespoons **mayonnaise** - depending on how moist you want it.

Shred cheddar on a grater and put in a medium mixing bowl. Add all the ingredients and mix well. Refrigerate.

CHICKEN OR TURKEY SALAD

INGREDIENTS:
1 cup shredded or chopped cooked **chicken** (or leftover turkey)
1/4 cup **chopped celery**
1 tablespoon finely **chopped onion**
2 tablespoons chopped **pecans, walnuts or slivered almonds**
2 **heaping** tablespoons **mayonnaise** (or more as you like it)
1/2 teaspoon **salt and pepper**
(option) 12 seedless **grapes** sliced in half
(option) 1/8 cup chopped **apple**

Mix all ingredients together and refrigerate.

TUNA SALAD

INGREDIENTS:
1, 5 ounce can **tuna well-drained** (open can and use the lid to squeeze out the liquid over the sink)
1/3 cup **chopped celery**
1 tablespoon finely **chopped onion**
2 **heaping** tablespoons **mayonnaise**
(option) 1/2 tablespoon **pickle relish** (sweet or dill)
(option) 1/2 of a **hard-boiled egg**, chopped

Mix all ingredients together and refrigerate.

EGG SALAD

INGREDIENTS: (1 serving)
2 hard-boiled **eggs**, peeled and chopped coarsely
1-1/2 tablespoon **celery** chopped fine
2 tablespoons **mayonnaise**
salt and **pepper**
plus any of the following options:
1 heaping tablespoon **shredded cheddar or Swiss cheese**, 1/2 teaspoon **mustard**, 1 teaspoon
   chopped fresh **parsley**, 1/4 teaspoon **dill**, 1/2 teaspoon chopped **chives**, 1/2 tablespoon finely
   chopped **green onion**

Mix all ingredients together and refrigerate or eat immediately.

BENEDICTINE

This cucumber-based spread was created in my home town. It's delicious on white or rye bread or rye toast as a sandwich spread or just some good crackers. You can also add a couple of strips of crisp bacon to make it an even tastier sandwich.

INGREDIENTS:
1, 8 ounce package **cream cheese** softened
1 **large cucumber**, peeled and seeded
1 teaspoon finely **grated onion**
1 teaspoon **dill**
dash of **salt**
(some people add one (and only one!) drop of green food coloring, but this is not necessary.)

1. Set out your cream cheese to soften. You can microwave it for 15 seconds to get it started - but remove the packaging first!

2. Peel and remove seed core of the cucumber. It's helpful to cut it in thirds so you can dig out the seeds more easily.

3. Using the finest, smallest teeth on a box grater, grate the the entire cucumber into a fine mesh strainer set in bowl. Pour the cucumber juice into another small bowl or cup and save.

4. Using the back of a large spoon or a spatula keep pressing the cucumber pulp against the strainer to remove the liquid. Do this over and over for a minute or two. You do not want the pulp to be too wet.

5. Add the cucumber pulp to the cream cheese. Grate the onion on the same side of the box grater and add it to the cream cheese. Add salt and dill and mix thoroughly. Add 2 tablespoons of the reserved cucumber juice and mix in.

6. Chill covered for a couple of hours.

TURKEY

Turkey is not just for Thanksgiving... well, maybe a whole turkey is! I cook a turkey breast every couple of months. I like having real turkey for sandwiches or turkey salad or a club sandwich in the summer when my home-grown tomatoes are ripe. I also use it to make Turkey Tetrazzini.

I like to use roasting bags — they are a clear plastic-like material. They keep the turkey very moist. You don't get a super-browned skin, but who needs that? You can always turn on the broiler after you remove it from the bag to give it extra browning if you want. You will need the large size bag for a turkey or the smaller ones for a breast. (You can also use them to roast a chicken, chuck roast or pork loin.)

THAWING
You will have to thaw the turkey. You will thaw it in the refrigerator. A whole turkey will take 3 or more days depending on size; a breast will take 2 days. See *Safe Thawing and Defrosting Methods.*

PREP
After you unpackage the turkey check the cavity for a bag of innards and maybe a bag of gravy. Some come with this stuff. Remove it. *If you are going to make dressing boil the innards in a little water for about 45 minutes and refrigerate the parts and the liquid. You can use or toss the gravy.*

Rinse the turkey inside and out under cold running water. Set it in a roasting pan. Salt and pepper it inside and out. Brush it with some melted butter. Place it in the roasting bag. **Read the roasting bag instructions for cooking times and temperature based on the weight of the turkey. Follow the instructions for prepping the bag - adding flour and cutting a few slits in it.**

If you don't use a roasting bag just set the turkey in the roasting pan (on a wire rack insert if you have one) and bake in a 325°F pre-heated oven: 8 to 12 pound **whole turkey** for 2-3/4 to 3 hours; 12 to 14 pounds for 3 to 3-3/4 hours. **Turkey breast:** 4 to 6 pounds for 1-1/2 to 2-1/4 hours; 6 to 8 pounds for 2-1/4 to 3-1/4 hours

Always use a **meat thermometer** to test for internal temperature of 165°F to be sure it is cooked. Insert probe in the inner thigh area near the breast, but not touching the bone. If you are not sure, make a cut between the thigh and breast. If the juices run clear it is done. If roasting a breast insert the probe into the center of the breast.

Let the turkey rest for at least 20 minutes after it is done. If you want to use the juices you will get from a whole turkey to make gravy you will need to pour them into a large gravy separator. Let the juices cool for 20 minutes, pour off the liquid and put the fat in a small bowl. See *Gravies, page 28.*

DRESSING
A simple, basic recipe... 2 servings.

1. 1/2 loaf of plain **white bread**. Place slices of bread on 2 baking sheets and place in a 225°F oven until the bread is dried out — 60-90 minutes. It should snap when you go to break it up. Turn it a few times while drying out. When dried break up the slices in small pieces and put them in a large mixing bowl.

2. Sauté 1 large chopped **onion** and 3 cups chopped **celery** in 4 tablespoons of **butter** in a large skillet until soft - about 15 minutes.

3. Add 1/2 tablespoon **poultry seasoning**, 1 teaspoon of **salt** and **pepper** and 1 can of **low-sodium chicken broth** to pan. Mix and bring to a simmer.

4. Once the mixture reaches a simmer turn off the heat. Pour mixture over bread and mix well. You may need additional broth to get it moist enough. You don't want it soupy or soggy — just slightly moist. Add more broth as needed, not necessarily a whole can.

5. Spread the mixture in a large, greased baking dish. Bake at 400°F, turning often, until browned and no longer doughy, but still moist — 45 - 60 minutes.

VEGETABLES

POTATOES

Potatoes fall into seven basic **varieties**: red, white, russet, yellow, blue/purple, petite and fingerling. You may see most of these at your market. Each variety has its own characteristics which makes them better for certain uses.

You don't want to choose a potato based on its color or shape or size. The most important characteristic for selecting a potato is its **starch content**. This is what determines a potato's best use. Starch content will determine if it will be light and fluffy when baked or hold its shape in a soup or a potato salad. Starch content also determines the **level of carbohydrates**. Avoid high starch potatoes if watching your carbs.

High-starch potatoes have a light, mealy texture. They're best for baking, mashing, and french-frying. Higher starch potatoes absorb water which causes them to fall apart when boiled – not good for potato salads.

Medium-starch potatoes are more moist than high-starch potatoes and hold their shape better.

Low-starch potatoes are the best for potato salads. They hold their shape better than other types.

RUSSET POTATOES / IDAHO POTATOES

Perhaps the most common in the American diet. These medium to large, oblong-shaped potatoes

have a **high starch** content and a thicker, tougher skin compared to other potatoes, but it is edible. Their flesh tends to be dry and flaky which causes them to fall apart easily if used in soups, stews and salads. *Best used for baking, frying, mashing.*

RED POTATOES

This variety of small to medium, round or slightly oblong potato, has a thin skin and is **low in starch**. The flesh is firm, moist and creamy. They hold together well when cooked or added to

dishes. You will often see their popular smaller cousin, red New Potatoes. You may also see a newer variety that is a hybrid between a red and Yukon Gold called **Butter Red** – red skin with a golden, buttery flesh. *Best used for boiling, roasting, mashing, pan-frying, potato salads, soups and stews.*

WHITE POTATOES

This variety of small to medium, round to long shaped potato, has a thin skin and is **low in starch**. Their skins do not need to re-moved for mashed

potatoes. Their flesh is slightly dense and creamy. *Best used for mashing, salads, steaming, boiling, pan-frying.*

FINGERLINGS

Fingerlings are basically an elongated variety of new potatoes, but with a thin finger-like shape. *Best used for roasting or using in potato salads with or without the skin.*

YUKON GOLDS

These golden skinned, oval shaped potatoes have a yellowish flesh, a rich and buttery flavor and a moist, creamy texture. A **medium starch** content makes them a good all-purpose potato suitable for most dishes though they tend to fall apart when cooked too long. They excel as mashed potatoes. *Best used for boiling, mashed potatoes, pan-frying and potato salad.*

NEW POTATOES

These 2 to 3 inch long potatoes are picked before reaching maturity which means their flavor is a bit more intensified. They look like miniature versions of their larger cousins - red, white and Yukon Gold. They generally have a waxier and creamier texture. They are **low in starch** and hold together well when cooked. Because they have thin skins they need not be peeled when eaten. *Best used for boiling, roasting, in soups or potato salads.*

CANNED POTATOES

Yes, these are not a variety of potato, but you do find canned potatoes either whole or sliced at the market. These are generally some variety of new potato packed in water. In a pinch they can be helpful. I always keep some in the pantry. The water leaches out a lot of their starch so they take a while to brown in a skillet. They work well for pan frying in a little butter or oil, boiling and tossing with some butter and fresh parsley or for adding to some long-cooking green beans – which is how you often see them.

WARNING !!!

If the potato has sprouted or the skin has a greenish hue do not eat it. These are signs that the potato is past its prime or has been subject to too much light which creates toxins in the potato. It can cause illness.

QUICK USE REFERENCE

Mashed Potatoes
russet/Idaho • white • red
yukon gold (most delicious)

Baked
Idaho/russet

Boiled/Steamed
white • red • new potatoes
yukon gold

French Fried
russet/Idaho • yukon gold

Pan Fried
white • red • Idaho/russet • fingerlings

Oven Roasted
red • white • new potatoes • yukon gold

Grilled
yukon gold • red • fingerlings • white

Soups
red • white• new potatoes • yukon gold

Potato Salad
(skins on or peeled)
red • fingerling • yukon gold
new potatoes

Gratins
(potato and cheese casseroles)
red • white • yukon gold

COOKING POTATOES

Here are some basic instructions for preparing potatoes in a variety of ways...

CLEAN: Always scrub the potato skin with a vegetable brush or your hands under cold water to remove any dried-on dirt. Yes, they are cleaned at the processing plant, but not always so well.

PREP: Cut off any **dark spots**. You don't want to cook bad spots. You might discover as you do this that that dark spot is bigger than a spot. It may run deep and be a sign of something more sinister - a bad potato. If the potato has started "sprouting" or has a greenish skin throw it out. (See *Warning* page 127.)

BAKING POTATOES

You would think anyone can bake a potato. Stick in oven and cook, right? That's the short of it, but there are things to keep in mind. So many people "bake" their potatoes in a microwave these days that many of them have a pre-timed button just for that. Baking cooks from the outside in while a microwave cooks by agitating every molecule at the same time creating heat. For most foods baking in an oven develops more flavor. Microwaves are great for reheating and some other tasks.

You can bake any kind of potato. Some are better for baking than others, so it's really up to you. The Idaho or russet is the general choice for baking because of its characteristics, but since they are high in carbs compared to other varieties you might want to select another type like a white, red, Yukon Gold.

OVEN METHOD: Scrub the skin with a vegetable brush then pat it dry so the skin get's crispy. If you like a soft skin rub it with some oil or butter. Poke 2 slits in the top with a knife about 1/2 inch deep. Place the potato in a 350°F oven and bake for about 60 minutes (400°F for about 45 minutes).The slower you cook it the better the texture. Size and variety of potato determines the length. You can always test it by inserting a knife (if there is any resistance at all it is not done) or use a meat thermometer that reads 210°F when it is done. There is a **quick-cook method** for a baked potato: cut the potato in half lengthwise. Score the flesh side in a diamond pattern, 1/4 inch deep cuts about an inch apart. Brush some oil on the flesh. Salt and pepper. Cook face down on a non-stick baking sheet. This takes half the time of a whole baked potato. Check it after 15 minutes to make sure it is not burning. If so, flip and cook until tender. This method also works great for **grilling**.

Should I wrap a potato in foil? This is not really baking - this is steaming in an oven. The water in the potato is trapped in the foil and basically steams it. You do not get a flaky interior or a crisp skin.

MICROWAVE METHOD: *DO NOT* use the "baked potato" setting on your microwave if it has one. I have yet to have a perfect baked potato from a microwave. They cook unevenly if you do not take a few extra simple steps. (Again, this is not really baking.) How often is one part of the potato "done" and another part seems hard or undone?

First, you have to create a deep slit in the top of the potato with a knife so it does not explode - a possible hazard when "baking" a potato in a microwave.

Secondly, you want to **cook it slowly.** I have found the best way to do this is to cook it for 1 minute. Let it rest for 2 minutes. Cook it for another minute and rest for 2 more. I continue to do this until it is done. This cooks it more slowly allowing the heat to spread throughout the potato more evenly. Yes, it takes longer, but your potato will be better off for it.

If you have one of those plastic **microwave plate domes** that you put over a plate of food when you reheat it, you can use that as well. This traps some heat and moisture.

Even though I am told wrapping foods in **plastic wrap** and cooking/reheating is bad (something to do with nasty chemicals in plastics that are vaporized when heated) I do like to wrap my potato for baking in the microwave. The potato seems more moist and cooks even MORE evenly. (Maybe I should try some parchment paper next time.) If you do this (and you have been warned about dangerous possible side-effects) be sure to make a deep slit in the potato and **cut a few small slits in the plastic wrap** for steam to escape – or you might have an explosion!

TWICE-BAKED POTATOES

Stuffed or loaded is another name for this recipe.

You will first bake (or microwave) your potato. After it cools cut off a thin layer from the top to expose the flesh. With a paring knife cut around the potato about 1/4 inch in from the side being careful not to break the skin or cut through the bottom. Now take a fork or spoon and gently dig out the flesh leaving some on the bottom to protect the skin. Place the flesh in a bowl.

Add some salt and pepper, grated cheddar, American or Velveeta cheese, a little sour cream, a little butter and some parsley or chives if you have them. You can add crumbled bacon if you like. Cover and microwave for about 1 minute or until the cheese starts to melt. Stir everything together. Leave it chunky or make it smooth.

Fill the potato skin with the mixture. Top with a dash of paprika. Bake in 350°F oven for 15 to 20 minutes until heated through.

BOILED POTATOES

The next most common method for cooking potatoes is boiling or steaming. This may be a prelude for creating something else, like making mashed potatoes, potato salad or a potato casserole or an end in itself – boiled potatoes with a little butter and fresh parsley is a common side dish.

Par-Boiling: Sometimes you will want to boil a potato for a short time, not to doneness, for use in other recipes like making home fries or a potato casserole. You will cut the potatoes in the shape needed and boil them in salted water for a few minutes - time is determined by size of the pieces. After they boil for a couple of minutes insert a knife into a piece of the potato – if it seems to be almost done, but still a bit hard in the middle you are done par-boiling.

Simple, Boiled Potatoes: Russets and Idahos can be boiled, but they are not ideal for this. Red, white and Yukon Golds are better for this purpose. Plus they have more taste. Scrub the skins; remove bad spots. If using large red or gold potatoes cut them in quarters or sixths. If using the small varieties leave them whole. Place them in a pot large enough to have about 1/2 inch of water over them. Salt the water. Potatoes require a lot of salt. If using the small red (new potatoes) or small Yukon gold potatoes you will often see a strip of the skin peeled from around the middle. This is done for looks only. Bring the pot to a medium boil and cook until done. Test them with a knife for doneness. Drain. If you used the small potatoes cut them in half before dressing them.

Dress with some butter, fresh parsley, pepper or even a little lemon juice.

MASHED POTATOES

Any variety of potato works well for mashing. If using russet or Idaho you will want to peel them first. The thin skin varieties like red or Yukon Gold don't have to be peeled if you don't mind skins in your mashed potatoes. Their skins are tender. The skins are nutritious. Slice the potatoes in 1/2 inch rings or 1 inch cubes. Place the potatoes in salted water, bring to a boil and cook until just tender. *Don't overcook* or they will become watery.

*NOTE: If you are tempted to use a **hand mixer** to make your mashed potatoes you must be VERY careful. Use low speed and only for a very short time. Over-whipping will cause them to get pasty and gluey. The ideal way is to use a kitchen tool called a "potato ricer." You put in the potatoes, turn the crank and they fall out mashed into the bowl. All you have to do is add some butter and warm milk and give them a stir with a spoon.*

Just before done warm some milk (or cream if you want decadent mashed potatoes). Drain the potatoes. Add some **butter, salt and pepper** and mash the butter into the potatoes. Add some **milk** and mash a little more. Now start whipping them with the masher or a large whisk. Add milk as needed to get them to a good consistency – not soupy, but thick and creamy. As soon as they are smooth, *STOP*. I repeat, over-whipping will cause them to get pasty and gluey. Taste for salt.

FRIED OR BAKED, POTATO WEDGES OR ROUNDS

Skillet method: You will start with a baked or microwaved potato with skin on. When it is done (for wedges) slice it in half lengthwise and slice each half in half lengthwise. Let it sit for 5 minutes, then slice each quarter in half lengthwise – you will have 8 wedges; for rounds, cut the potato is 3/8 inch rings and let them sit for 5 minutes. Letting them rest will give them a better crust when fried.

Add a few tablespoons of oil to a skillet set on medium high heat. Place the pieces of potato in the skillet and brown well on both sides until crispy. Adjust skillet heat as necessary. Add salt and pepper at the end.

Oven method: Preheat oven to 425°F. Slice raw potatoes in 3/8 inch rounds with skin on. Place the rounds in a pile on a non-stick baking sheet. Drizzle with some oil, salt and pepper. Toss to coat. Spread them out evenly in the sheet. Bake for 15 minutes then remove from the oven and flip them over. Check them in 15 minutes for doneness. They should be brown and crispy but soft in the center.

HOME FRIES

These are similar to the Pan-Fried potatoes above. You can start with raw potatoes or pre-baked or parboiled. If you start with raw potatoes you will have to steam them a bit in a covered skillet to speed up the cooking. Some people like to add sliced onion to their home fries. Just peel and slice some onion and put it in the skillet with the potatoes.

Using raw potatoes: Home fries are usually cut into cube-like pieces. Cut potato in half, then each half in half, etc., until you have pieces about one inch square-ish. *You will find that one potato, after fried this way, looks like you cooked a half of a potato – they shrink a lot using this method. You may want to use 2 medium size potatoes instead of 1 large per person.* Rinse the pieces in cold water and pat dry. Put a few tablespoons of oil in a skillet on medium heat. Put in the potatoes and toss to coat. Cover and cook, stirring every few minutes. When they are soft, remove the lid, add some salt and pepper and continue to fry until they are crisp and brown.

Using pre-cooked potatoes: Start with a baked potato or par-boiled potatoes. If you par-boil make sure to drain them well and let them sit and air-dry for about 5 minutes or they will not brown well. Cut potato in half, then each half in half, etc., until you have pieces about one inch square-ish. *You will find that one potato, after fried this way, looks like you cooked a half of a potato – they shrink a lot using this method. You may want to use 2 medium size potatoes instead of 1 large per person..* Put a few tablespoons of oil in a skillet on medium heat. Put in the potatoes, add some salt and pepper and toss to coat. Turn the potatoes every few minutes until they are crispy and browned.

German Fried potatoes are very similar, only the cut is different. You slice the potatoes in 1/4 inch rounds and then cut the rounds into halves or fourths. They are cooked raw, not par-boiled or pre-baked. They take quite a while to brown and get done and need lots of turning.

OVEN ROASTED POTATOES

Roasting raw potatoes in the oven is a simple way to prepare potatoes especially when feeding several people or a crowd. The small new potatoes, either the red skin or Yukon Gold variety, work especially well as they remain more moist whereas russets tend to be dry.

Preheat oven to 450°F. If using the small new potatoes just cut them in half and place them on a non-stick baking sheet. If using a larger red or Yukon or russet, cut them into quarters or sixths or eighths depending on size. Place them on a rimmed cookie sheet and drizzle with oil (olive or other), salt and pepper and toss them well to coat. Spread them out into a single layer. (You can add a little rosemary or cayenne pepper or garlic powder as well.) Bake for 30 minutes then turn them over. Bake for another 15 minutes or so – type of potato and size determines doneness. Taste for salt and pepper when done. *TIP: For a crispier exterior you will parboil the cut potatoes first in salted water with a tablespoon of vinegar for 5 minutes. When done, drain, let air dry for a few minutes, then drizzle with plenty of oil, add some salt and pepper and stir them around so some of the flesh breaks up and coats the skins. Then bake as above with no additional oil.*

FRENCH FRIES

Who doesn't like French fries? To make the best fries takes a bit of time. The best fries are fried twice. If you have a fryer, great – skip to the next paragraph. You can also use a heavy pot like a Dutch Oven. Do not use a pot with a non-stick coating for frying. If using a pot you will need a candy or deep-frying thermometer attached to the side of the pot. The tip should stay at least 1/4 inch from the bottom of the pot. You will need several inches of vegetable or canola oil. *Make sure you have 3 inches of space above the oil to the top of the pot as the oil will rise when the fries are added.*

Cut your potatoes into fries. Rinse cut potatoes in a large bowl with lots of cold running water until water becomes clear – you are washing off the starch. Cover with water by 1-inch and cover with ice. Refrigerate at least 30 minutes.

Heat oil over medium heat until the thermometer registers 325°F, or use the settings on your deep fryer.

Meanwhile, drain ice water from cut fries and wrap potato pieces in a clean dishcloth or tea towel and thoroughly pat dry. Increase the heat to medium-high and add fries, a handful at a time, to the hot oil. Fry, stirring occasionally, until potatoes are soft and limp and begin to turn a blond color, about 6 to 8 minutes. They should not get brown in this first frying. They should begin to look translucent. They will be limp. Using a skimmer or a slotted spoon, carefully remove fries from the oil and set aside to drain on paper towels. Turn off the heated oil. Let the fries rest for at least 20 minutes or up to 2 hours.

When ready to serve the fries, reheat the oil to 350°F. Transfer the blanched potatoes to the hot oil and fry again, stirring frequently, until golden brown and puffed, about 1 or 2 minutes. Transfer to paper towel to drain and sprinkle with salt and pepper, to taste. Serve immediately.

Potatoes au Gratin

A "gratin" is classically a dish made with a breadcrumb and cheese topping. However, in our American bent for excess we aren't satisfied with a little cheese on top! "Gratin" now often means made with lots of cheese. My favorite way to eat potatoes is this cheesy casserole of scalloped potatoes.

Time: 60 minutes
Servings: 4
Prep & Tools: 9" by 9" baking dish or equivalent

INGREDIENTS:

4 large **red potatoes peeled and sliced in 1/8 inch thick rounds.** (A mandolin slicer is perfect for this.

4 tablespoons of **butter**

3 tablespoons of **flour**

2 cups **cold milk**

1-1/2 cups grated **cheddar** or equivalent of American cheese or a 2-1/2 inch thick slice of **Velveeta cut into small cubes.** (my personal favorite for this recipe).

salt and **pepper**

(optional) 1/2 cup diced **red bell pepper**

(optional) 3 slices of fried **bacon** chopped

DIRECTIONS:

Preheat oven to 400°F.

1. Peel potatoes, slice, and par-boil them in a large pot of salted water. Boil for about 5-7 minutes just to tender. Remove from heat and drain.

2. Make a roux: in a medium saucepan melt butter on medium heat. Add flour and mix and cook for 2 minutes stirring constantly. Add 1/2 cup of the cold milk and stir until it is thick and smooth. Add another 1/2 cup of the cold milk and stir until it is thick and smooth. Add the rest of the milk and stir until it is smooth. Continue to stir mixture on medium heat until it begins to bubble and thicken. Remove from heat.

3. Add the cheese and stir to melt. Taste. Add more cheese if you want it cheesier.

4. Grease your baking dish with some butter. Spread 1/2 of the potatoes in the dish in a layer. Sprinkle with a little salt and pepper. (If using bell pepper and/or bacon sprinkle 1/2 on the layer.) Pour on 1/2 of the cheese sauce. Repeat for another layer. Top with a little paprika.

5. *You might want to place the baking dish on a baking sheet to catch any boil-over.* Cover dish with lid or foil and bake for 20 minutes or it begins to bubble. Remove cover and continue to bake for 25 more minutes, more or less, until the top is golden brown. If the potatoes are not tender and the top is brown, re-cover and cook until done.

Sweet Potatoes and Yams

Sweet potatoes and yams are actually two very different vegetables. However we have come to use the terms interchangeably. Sweet potatoes have an elongated body and tapered ends. Their skin may be yellow or orange with flesh the same color. The darker orange sweet potato, often called a yam in error, has a more sweet flesh and a moisture texture than its yellowish counterpart. It is the most common sweet potato you find at the market.

Yams are a tuber of a tropical vine and are sweeter than a sweet potato. Yams often have a brownish skin that looks like tree bark with off-white, purple or red flesh depending on the variety. There are many varieties and some that look very similar to sweet potatoes. Assume you are buying sweet potatoes at your local market even if the sign says "yams." Yams are usually found in specialty or international markets.

Orange-fleshed sweet potatoes are high in beta-carotene. Recent studies have shown that sweet potatoes raise our blood levels of vitamin A. They also are good at regulating blood sugar levels. The purple variety are an especially good source for anti-oxidant offering much more than blueberries.

We should eat more sweet potatoes!

BUYING
Choose firm sweet potatoes without cracks, bruises or soft spots. Stay away from those displayed in a refrigerated case because cold degrades them.

KEEPING THEM FRESH
Sweet potatoes should be stored in a cool, dark and well-ventilated place, where they will keep fresh for up to ten days. Ideally, they should be kept out of the refrigerator. Keep them loose in a bin, never in a plastic bag, or in an open brown paper bag in a cool, dark, and well-ventilated cupboard away from sources of excess heat like the stove or oven.

The flesh of sweet potatoes will darken upon contact with the air. You need to cook them immediately after peeling and/or cutting them. If this isn't possible keep them in a bowl covered completely with water until you are ready to cook them to prevent oxidation.

STEAMING

1. Peel the potato and cut into 1/2-inch slices, then cut the slices in half or cut them into 1 inch cubes.

2. Steam them for about 7 minutes. This not only brings out their flavor, but maximizes their nutritional value. When done, toss them with a little cinnamon or nutmeg and butter.

BAKING

1. Preheat oven to 450°F.

2. Scrub sweet potato under running water and dry well with paper towel.

3. Poke all over with fork.

4. Place sweet potatoes on some foil on a cookie sheet and bake for 30 minutes.

5. Flip over and set timer for 30 more minutes, 20 minutes if they are smaller (shorter than your palm). Remove, scrape off any blackened crusties from the leaking juices.

6. When done, let it cool for about 5 minutes – until you can touch it without getting burned! Split down the middle, give it a squeeze to open it up like a regular baked

You can add any of the following or nothing at all: a little butter (they do not need much), cinnamon, honey, nutmeg, ginger, maple syrup, brown sugar, chopped pecan or walnuts, coconut milk...

TWICE BAKED

Bake the sweet potato. Scoop out the flesh into a bowl – leaving about 1/4 inch of flesh on the skin. Add some butter, cinnamon, pecans, brown sugar or honey and mash together. Spoon back into skin. Bake in oven at 400°F for 15 to minutes until heated through.

ROASTING

1. Preheat oven to 375°F.

2. Peel the sweet potato and cut it in 1 inch cubes. Place the cubes in a pile on a rimmed baking sheet. (You could also cut them into French Fries shape.)

3. Drizzle with some oil, honey, cinnamon, a little salt and pepper and toss to coat.

4. Spread them out in an even layer.

5. Bake for about 25 to 30 minutes until tender, turning once or twice during cooking.

MASHED/WHIPPED

1. Peel and boil the potatoes until tender. Drain.

2. Add some orange juice, a little butter and cinnamon.

3. Mash with a potato masher. You can leave them chunky or whip them smooth.

PAN-SAUTÉED

1. Peel a potato and cut in 1/2 inch rings.

2. Place in a skillet large enough to hold all the rings in a single layer and add enough water so it is about 1/8 inch deep.

3. Cover skillet and simmer for about 10 minutes.

4. Uncover skillet, flip rings over and simmer until water is evaporated.

5. Now add some butter and 3 tablespoons of apricot preserves or orange marmalade or brown sugar. Stir to mix. Let the potatoes simmer, turning often until they are browned on both sides.

SWEET POTATO CASSEROLE

2 servings. Use a 9 inch by 9 inch baking dish or something equivalent in size at least 3 inches deep.

1. Peel and slice 2 large or 3 medium sweet potatoes in 1/4 inch slices. Use a mandolin slicer if you have one.

2. Par-boil the sweet potatoes: place the slices in a pot of salted water, bring to a boil and boil for 3 minutes. Drain and set aside.

3. In a saucepan mix together:
   4 tablespoon melted butter
   1/4 cup maple syrup or orange juice
   1/4 cup orange marmalade or apricot
      preserves
   1/2 teaspoon cinnamon
   1 tablespoon rum or bourbon or an
      orange-flavored liqueur
   2 tablespoons chopped pecans or walnuts

4. Grease baking dish with butter. Make a layer of potatoes using half of the slices and pour half of the mixture over them. Make another layer using remaining slices and and pour rest of mixture over them.

5. Cover and bake at 400°F for 30 minutes. Test for tenderness with a knife. Cook longer if necessary to reach tenderness.

BROCCOLI & CAULIFLOWER

These two vegetables are very similar is ways they can be cooked - steamed, roasted, sautéed, used in a stir-fry, casserole, soup or salad or eaten raw. Using **fresh** broccoli or cauliflower is the ideal as the **frozen** versions turn to mush when cooked. Another vegetable that one might think is related is **broccolini**. It may be cooked the same way as broccoli and cauliflower. *See next page.*

 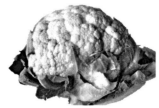

What to Look for When You Buy

Obviously, never buy these veggies if they look old. Cauliflower with get brownish spots; broccoli will get yellowish patches. Never buy broccoli that is limp. When you are ready to cook these veggies and there are some bad spots just cut it off.

Keeping It Fresh

If you buy these vegetables at a typical grocery you have no idea how long it has been since they were harvested. Sometimes they begin to wilt and feel rubbery in a matter of days once you get them home. You do not want to cook it or use it in this condition. When this happens I cut off the florets, place them in a covered container and cover them with water. After a day of re-hydrating in the refrigerator they will spring back to firmness. You can then drain off the water and keep them sealed in the container. (This re-hydration works for most vegetables – bell peppers, asparagus, carrots, celery!) Now, I have heard you should never seal veggies in a bag or container because they should breathe, but the above method has worked for me for many years and I have had no problems. I have even left them in the fridge in water for several days before draining them.

STEAMING

The saucepan you use for steaming must have a lid. If you have a **steamer insert** for a saucepan, either the kind that sits in the bottom of a pot and folds out or a pot with bottom holes that sits within another pot - these are ideal for steaming, but a plain pot with a lid will work as well. You will add about **1/4 inch of lightly salted water** to the pot and place the veggies in the receptacle part or just into the pot and **cover**. They will not be sitting in a pot full of water. If you want you can use pieces of the inedible parts to line the bottom of the pot to hold up the florets out of the water altogether. Of course, these have to be removed if you are going to drain the pot and melt some butter over them.

Ideally, you can *steam these veggies just minutes before you are ready to eat/serve them.* Cooking them in advance will lead to them being over-done.

So:

1. Put your water and a little salt in your pot.

2. With the lid on your saucepan turn the burner to high.

3. When steam begins to escape around the edge of the lid turn down the heat to medium-low.

4. Set your timer: depending on the size you cut the florets broccoli will take no more than 2 to 3 minutes and cauliflower no more than 3 to 4 minutes.. If you are unfamiliar with steaming veggies set it for the lowest number, test the veggies with a knife. If done, drain the pot, but **do not re-cover it** as the heat from the veggies will continue to steam them and they will be overdone. If they are still too hard, re-cover the pot and steam for one more minute.

Doneness

They should be firm when done. Broccoli should remain **bright green** and cauliflower **white**, not grayish. A knife inserted in the thickest part of the stem part of the floret will tell you if they are done.

Serving

While the drained florets are in the pot add a little **butter** or margarine and/or **lemon juice**. Toss to coat. You could also add a little grated **parmesan cheese** or **lemon zest**.

ROASTING (15-20 minutes)

Roasting these veggies brings out more flavor as this method caramelizes the natural sugars in them.

1. Place the **dry**, never wet, **florets** on a nonstick baking sheet or pie pan.
2. Drizzle a tablespoon of any type of oil, (or more depending on how much you are roasting) over the florets.
3. Sprinkle with a little salt.
4. Toss the florets in the oil.
5. Place in a 425°F oven. After 10 minutes toss them again and roast for 5 more minutes give them a knife test and cook more if needed. The edges should be slightly browned.

When done, put the florets in a bowl, toss with some melted butter or lemon juice or both. You could also add some lemon zest or grated parmesan or cheddar cheese.

GRILLING

These veggies can also be grilled - which is similar to roasting them. Place the florets in a bowl, toss with a little oil and salt to coat. Place them on the grill in a grilling pan or plate – the kind with holes in the bottom. Time will depend on the temperature of your grill. Turn them once or twice in the process. Don't grill them over flames as they will char.

When done, put the florets in a bowl, toss with some melted butter or lemon juice or both. You could also add some lemon zest or grated parmesan or cheddar cheese.

IN A SALAD

Bite-size bits of these veggies can be added to a salad raw, but you can **blanche** them to slightly soften them. Steam some florets for 3 minutes. Immediately after you drain them put them in a bowl of **cold water** *with ice*. Let them sit for 5 minutes and drain. This stops the cooking and locks in the color. Then chop them up a little smaller and add to your salad.

BROCCOLINI

A Chinese vegetable, also known as sprouting broccoli. It is a hybrid vegetable, not specific to just the broccoli family, nor is it baby broccoli  (that is what is what resembles, though). They are spear shaped, with thin and tender vibrant green stems with lengths that rarely exceed 6" long. The head is a loose small cluster of florets that resemble broccoli. Compared to the common broccoli, the flavor is understated, mild, peppery and subtly sweet. The entire plant is edible.

ROASTED CAULIFLOWER *or broccoli* WITH LEMON & PARMESAN

Time: 20 minutes
Servings: 1
Tools: rimmed non-stick cookie sheet, cake pan or pie pan

INGREDIENTS:

1 serving of **cauliflower or broccoli** florets

1 tablespoon **olive oil**

1 tablespoon **lemon juice**

1 **garlic** clove, minced

1/4 teaspoon **salt**

1/4 teaspoon **pepper**

1 tablespoon freshly grated **parmesan cheese** (best to use the good stuff, Parmigiana-Reggiano)

DIRECTIONS:

1. Preheat oven to 475°F. On your roasting pan of choice, toss cauliflower pieces with olive oil, lemon juice, garlic, salt and pepper.

2. Roast for 15 minutes, stirring occasionally, until crisp tender and lightly browned.

3. Transfer to a serving dish and sprinkle with parmesan cheese.

BROCCOLI (OR CAULIFLOWER) WITH CHEESE FOR ONE

Cheese just adds something special to broccoli or cauliflower. This recipe is how to make a single serving without the fuss of making a cheese sauce or casserole.

Time: 10 minutes
Tools: saucepan to steam broccoli, ice bath, serving bowl

INGREDIENTS: a serving of broccoli or cauliflower florets, 1 tablespoon of breadcrumbs, a few slices of American cheese or Velveeta or some grated cheddar, you make it as cheesy as you like!

DIRECTIONS: 1. Steam the broccoli or cauliflower just enough to tender - 2 -3 minutes. Immediately drain and put the florets in a bowl of cold water and ice for 5 minutes to stop the cooking. **2.** Put the breadcrumbs in the bottom of your serving bowl for one. Place the drained veggies on top. Cover the top with the cheese. **3.** Microwave the dish for 1 minute and let it rest for 1 minute. Microwave for another minute. Repeat until the cheese has melted. **4.** The veggies will give off water in this process. The breadcrumbs will absorb it and any cheese that reaches the bottom of the bowl. Stir it all up to spread the cheese throughout. *You could instead put this under the broiler for a short time to melt the cheese, just use a broiler-safe bowl.*

BROCCOLI *or cauliflower* CHEESE CASSEROLE

This is not a fancy casserole - it's a soup-based, home-style kind of thing.

Time: 45 minutes
Servings: 4
Prep & Tools: rimmed non-stick cookie sheet, cake pan or pie pan

INGREDIENTS:

1 large head of broccoli or cauliflower cut into florets. (about 4 cups)

1 can cream of broccoli soup (or celery soup if using cauliflower) or cream of mushroom soup.

1/2 cup milk

1 inch thick slice of **Velveeta or 8 slices of American cheese or 1 cup grated cheddar or 1 cup grated parmesan**

1 cup **cracker crumbs** (either from a box or just crunch up your own). You can use saltines, Ritz, Townhouse crackers, etc....

DIRECTIONS:

Preheat oven to 450°F.

1. Steam the broccoli or cauliflower just enough to begin it cooking - 2 minutes for broccoli, 3 for cauliflower. Immediately drain and put the florets in a bowl of cold water and ice to stop the cooking.

2. In a small saucepan heat the soup, then add the milk and mix well. Now add the cheese and simmer until it melts.

3. Spray a large baking dish with cooking spay or rub it with some butter. Sprinkle half of the cracker crumbs over the bottom.

4. Place the broccoli/cauliflower in a layer in the dish. Sprinkle remaining crumbs on top. Pour the sauce over evenly. Jiggle the dish to help the sauce settle down into the cracks and crevices.

5. Cover and put in the oven. Turn the temp down to 400°F. After about 20 minutes check to see if it is bubbling. When it bubbles remove the cover and bake for another 20 or so minutes until it begins to brown.

6. Let it sit for about 10 minutes before serving so it can set.

BROCCOLI-RICE OR BROCCOLI-NOODLE CHEESY CASSEROLE

This makes a standard broccoli-cheese casserole into a double-duty recipe - a vegetable and a starch.

Same as above, but: use only 1/2 cup cracker crumbs; you will need 2 cups of cooked rice or cooked egg noodles or pasta like macaroni or ziti. You will need 1 cup of milk. Make the soup/milk/cheese base in a large saucepan. Then add the cooked broccoli/cauliflower and cooked rice or noodles to the pot and mix it all together. Pour it into your greased baking dish and top with the cracker crumbs.

ASPARAGUS

Asparagus is a quick-cooking vegetable and there are many ways to prepare it: steamed, pan sautéed, baked, broiled and grilled. If you overcook it asparagus gets limp and mushy. The thickness of the spears will determine how long you cook it. It is something you need to keep an eye on while cooking it. If asparagus turns an olive green they are probably overcooked. Perfectly cooked asparagus retains a bright green color.

If you are not used to cooking fresh asparagus, one or two experiences will teach you how long it generally takes depending on the thickness of the spears.

Buying: Choose stalks and tips that are firm, not limp. The feathery tips should be tight, not loose.

Storing: Cut about 1/4 inch off the bottom of the stalks. Place the asparagus in a glass, tips up, with about 1/2 inch of water in the glass. Or you can place them in a plastic bag with a wet paper towel.

Uses: Besides eating asparagus as a side vegetable they are great for adding to other dishes like a stir-fry, hot or cold pasta dishes and salads.

PREP THE SPEARS
Asparagus has a tough, woody end and it should be removed before cooking. *Always do this before cooking*. Take a spear in your hand placing the fingers of one hand at the end of the spear and the fingers of your other hand in the middle of the spear. Bend the spear until it snaps. This is an easy method for removing that part of the spear that would be tough and woody

when cooked. Keep the removed ends - you can use them for steaming if using a saucepan.

STEAMING
If you have a steamer use that, if not, you can use a saucepan.

Using a steamer: Place about a 1/4 inch of salted water in your steamer. Cover, bring to a boil. Check them after a minute by inserting a knife into the thickest part of a spear. Thin spears cooks very quickly.

Using a saucepan: Place the woody stems you removed in the bottom of the pan. Add water about half way up the end pieces - do not cover them with water. Add a little salt. Place your spears on top. Cover and bring to a boil. Check them after a minute by inserting a knife into the thickest part of a spear. Thin spears cooks very quickly. Don't eat the woody stems!

PAN SAUTÉING
This works best with thin spears – pencil size and smaller. Place enough water in a small skillet just to cover the bottom ever so thinly - about 1/8 inch. Add a little butter, salt and pepper. Place the spears in the pan and bring to a boil. As soon as the water evaporates reduce the heat to low - they are probably done or close to it. Just test by sticking a sharp knife mid-spear.

ROASTING
Set oven to 400°F. Place the spears on a baking sheet. Drizzle with a little oil or melted butter and salt and pepper. Toss and spread them out on the sheet. Again, depending on the size they may take from 5 minutes to 15 minutes. You may want to turn them half way through the cooking. You could add some sliced almonds to them about 2 minutes before they are done. When finished, remove them to a platter or plate and drizzle with some lemon juice.

BROILING

Set the oven rack at it's highest position. Turn on the broiler. Wait for it to get hot. Place the spears on a baking sheet. Drizzle with a little oil or melted butter and salt and pepper. Toss and spread them out on the sheet. Depending on the size they may take from 3 minutes to 7 minutes. They will cook much faster than baking since broiling is a more direct heat. You want to turn them half way through the cooking. If they begin to burn, move them to a lower rack, turn off the boiler, close the oven door and let them sit in the hot oven to finish cooking.

GRILLING

Toss spears in a little oil, salt and pepper. Place on the grill, not over flame, and watch closely, turning occasionally. When they just start to get a bit limp they are done.

ADDING TO SALADS

When adding asparagus to something like a salad you want to blanch it first — boil it in salted water for a minute or two just to barely tender then place it in a cold water ice bath to stop the cooking. After 5 minutes remove, drain and cut into bite sizes for adding to a salad.

SERVING:

Asparagus can be topped with:

- sliced almonds (preferably "toasted" in a frying fan for a minute or two),

- melted butter

- some fresh squeezed lemon juice and lemon zest

- Hollandaise sauce

ASPARAGUS AND PEPPERS

Red, yellow or orange bell peppers make a good accompaniment to asparagus.

Slice some 4 inch long narrow strips of bell pepper. In a skillet on medium heat, add a little oil or butter. Toss in the pepper strips, toss to coat and sauté, turning often, for a couple of minutes. When they are almost done (you want them to have some tooth) toss in the asparagus spears. *If they are thick spears just put them in the pan with the peppers at the beginning.* Sprinkle with some salt and pepper. Sauté, turning often, until asparagus is just tender. Add some lemon juice.

MARINATED COLD ASPARAGUS

This was my father's favorite way to eat asparagus. First you need to prep it and blanch it — boil it in salted water for a minute or two just to barely tender then place it in a cold water and ice bath to stop the cooking. After 5 minutes remove and place the spears in a dish or on a plate where you can get them in a single layer. Pour over some Italian dressing, cover and let them marinate for at least an hour in the fridge. Serve them over some fresh salad greens or eat by themselves. The marinade on the spears will also dress the greens.

Brussels Sprouts

Sprouts have become more popular in the past few years. They are a member of the cabbage family. Steamed, they are touted to be the **ultimate vegetable for lowering cholesterol**. Like other cruciferous vegetables – broccoli, cauliflower, cabbage, radishes, arugula, turnip greens, they have **high cancer-preventive components**. Like broccoli and cauliflower, you get the most benefits by eating them raw, but steaming them just to tender retains most of their nutrients.

Fresh sprouts have a mild cabbage-like flavor, whereas old ones will be strong and even bitter. This explains why many people turn up their noses at them – they have never had fresh ones prepared well. If you overcook them they can also get strong and bitter.

BUYING
Fresh sprouts have a bright color and the outer leaves should not look old or wilted. If you can find a fresh market where you pick as many as you need right off their growing stalk, that's ideal. (Did you even know they were grown on a stalk?) Try to pick **the same size** so they will cook in the same amount of time.

KEEPING THEM FRESH
If you're sprouts begin to lose color or freshness, cut off about 1/4 inch of their stems, put them in a bowl, cover them with water and let them refrigerate. This can bring them back to life.

PREPPING
Before eating or cooking you need to cut off about 1/4 inch or so of the hard stem where they were attached to the stalk. They can be cooked whole or cut in half. Whenever you cut them some outer leaves will fall off and that's fine. Just discard any that look bad.

Sprouts can be steamed, roasted, pan sautéed, boiled or grilled. They caramelize well which means their sugars will brown.

RAW

Sprouts are very hard like broccoli and cauliflower. You can cut them in half and eat them raw, but it is probably better to work them raw, sliced thinly, into something else....

Slaw: Remove the hard stems and slice them thinly and add some to a cabbage slaw.

Sprouts Slaw: Remove the hard stems, slice them thinly and dress with a little oil and vinegar, salt, pepper, lemon juice and a little sugar or honey. Or use them instead of cabbage in a mayonnaise based slaw.

SOUPS

Add some sliced or quartered to a vegetable soup or cabbage soup.

STEAMING

Remove the hard stems. You can steam them in a salted water either whole or halved. Some may be much larger than others which is a good reason to at least halve the largest ones so the halves are about the same size as small ones. This allows them to finish cooking at the same time. It also makes dressing them and eating them a bit easier. **Steam until just tender - 4 to 5 minutes. No more or they get too soft and strong.**

Dress steamed sprouts with one or more of the following:
- butter
- extra-virgin olive oil
- balsamic vinegar

- fresh pepper
- a little honey
- a little warmed orange marmalade
- pecans or walnuts
- crumbled bacon

ROASTING

Remove the hard stems. Some may be much larger than others which is a good reason to at least halve the largest ones so the halves are about the same size as small ones. This allows them to finish cooking at the same time.

Preheat oven to 400°F. Place them in a bowl. drizzle over a little oil (canola or olive), and sprinkle with salt and pepper. Toss. Pour them onto a rimmed baking sheet. Roast for 20 to 30 minutes. Turn them a few times along the way. Test with a sharp knife for doneness - just tender.

Put in a bowl and toss with a little butter, or lemon or balsamic vinegar or all three.

Variation: Dice up a strip or two of bacon. Finely dice some onion. Add these to the bowl above. When done toss with a little balsamic vinegar.

GRILLING

Remove the hard stems. Some may be much larger than others which is a good reason to at least halve the largest ones so the halves are about the same size as small ones. This allows them to finish cooking at the same time.

Place them in a bowl. drizzle over a little oil (canola or olive), and sprinkle with salt and pepper. Toss. You will need to put them on a perforated grill plate or some aluminum foil on the grill. Cook until just tender.

Put in a bowl and toss with a little butter, or lemon or balsamic vinegar or all three.

PAN-SAUTÉING

Remove the hard stems. Some may be much larger than others which is a good reason to at least halve the largest ones so the halves are about the same size as small ones. This allows them to finish cooking at the same time.

Put an 1/8 inch of water in a skillet. Add the sprouts. Turn the heat to high and bring the water to a boil. Reduce heat but keep it boiling. This will steam the sprouts and get them cooking. Once the water is evaporated add enough oil to coat the sprouts, some salt and pepper, and pan-fry on medium heat just until they begin to brown.

Put in a bowl and toss with a little butter, or lemon or balsamic vinegar or all three.

BRUSSELS SPROUTS with BACON and VINEGAR

1. Fry a strip or two of **bacon** (depends on how many servings of sprouts you are making). Remove bacon to a paper towel to drain and reserve 1 or 2 tablespoons of bacon fat in the skillet and discard the rest.
2. Add a tablespoon or 2 of **butter** and a tablespoon or 2 of **oil**.
3. Finely dice a few tablespoons of **onions**. Add **halved sprouts** and onions to the pan and cook on medium heat, turning often.
4. When they begin to brown give them a test for doneness.
5. When done add a splash of **balsamic vinegar** or lemon juice and the bacon crumbled to the pan and toss well. Serve.

Green Beans

I must admit that I do not eat enough green beans. It is probably due to the fact that I most often buy canned green beans. Canned beans are fairly tasteless is you just boil them and add a little butter. They always seem to be missing something. I do like the Southern-style beans that are cooked for a few hours with a ham hock or ham bone, but as vegetables go, they can get really soft from all that simmering. At that point any nutrients are all but gone.

In the past few years I have become more accustomed to buy a handful of fresh green beans and only cook them for a short time. They have some crunch and I feel like I am actually eating something healthy and tasty. You will not find a recipe for the ever-present green bean casserole here. I detest it.

TYPES
There are basically 2 kinds of beans we find at the market: **green beans**, also called string or snap beans, and **French beans** (*haricot vert*). French beans are more slender than green beans and are slightly sweeter. I prefer them, and since they are more slender, they take even less time to cook. At the market they are usually bagged, not in an open bin like green beans, and they cost more.

KEEPING THEM FRESH
Obviously when you are selecting fresh green beans from a bin you want to choose those that are free of blemishes or are limp. If you get them home and they get limp before you are ready to use them just cover them with water and refrigerate. This will perk them right up.

PREPPING FRESH BEANS
First, **rinse** the beans several times in cold water.

Most fresh green beans at the market today are not string beans. They have managed to breed that nasty gene out of the them, but I still find some strings. (There is nothing worse than one of those tough stringy threads in your mouth.) You will find strings on beans that were not picked when they were young, but allowed to stay on the vine too long. At the market you never know how old the beans were when they were picked. When you buy beans read the label and avoid "string beans" varieties if you can.

A bean has two ends – the flatter end where it was attached to the vine and the end that is tapered at the end. You need to snap off or cut away the tail ends and that little stem that connected it to the plant. If you don't know if they have strings, just grab the end with your fingers and snap it and as you do so pull it down the back of the bean where there is a slight furrow - like peeling a banana. If there is a string it should pull off with the snapped end. If you find strings on some of the first ones it's best to de-string them all.

French beans should not have strings, but again, you don't know at what stage they were harvested.

CANNED GREEN BEANS
You will find several varieties of beans in cans at the market: cut green beans, whole green beans, Italian broad beans, French style beans, to name a few. I avoid the French style if using canned. They are mush. I think canned beans work best for longer cooking. Their flavor is very strong and longer cooking tends to mellow them.

If you can find canned whole green beans always use them. They are much better than cut green beans.

COOKING FRESH BEANS

Fresh beans need to be **blanched** – boiled in salted water for a short amount of time before finishing them by some other means. Usually 4 minutes is sufficient. This starts the cooking process. If you are only cooking a small serving you can blanche them in a small skillet. Just cover them with some salted water.

Once blanched they are put into a **cold water bath** to stop the cooking and set their bright green color. (You can use cold tap water.) After they sit in the cold water bath for about 5 minutes drain them and add fresh cold water and let them sit another few minutes. Drain and place them on a paper towel and **dry them off**. *If you boiled them in a skillet, just drain the water off the skillet and do a cold tap water exchange in the skillet - no need to dirty another bowl.*

Put a little oil (or bacon fat) in a skillet on medium heat. Toss in the beans, add some salt and pepper and toss to coat. Toss them frequently and sauté them for another 5 minutes.

Additions:
- Add a little minced **garlic** to the pan if you wish and/or some minced **onion** or **shallots**.

- Sliced **almonds** are a classic addition.

- **Lemon zest** is another nice addition.

- One of my favorite things to add to the beans are some thin slices of **red bell pepper** – their sweetness balances the "greeness" of the beans.

- Fresh sliced **mushrooms** add a nice earthiness.

- Crumbled **bacon** is always tasty!

- You can finish them by adding a little **butter** or a squeeze of fresh **lemon juice** just at the end or a drizzle of **olive oil**.

STEAMING

Of course, like most vegetables, you can steam fresh beans in salted water. Test them after 5 minutes and continue to steam until just tender. You can then dress them with any of the above additions.

COOKING CANNED BEANS

You don't have to cook canned beans a long time as they are somewhat tender already due to the canning process, but like I said before they have a stronger flavor that mellows with long cooking.

Beans, whether canned or fresh, need a fair amount of salt and pepper. I like the Italian broad beans, wider and flatter than green beans. I think they have more flavor, but I know many people who do not care for them for some reason.

Open the canned beans, **discard the water** and **rinse**. The water is very strong and you don't want to cook them in it.

Long-cooked Beans:

If you plan on using a smoked ham hock or a hambone read below, otherwise skip to *Recipe for 1 can of beans on the next page.*

The best long-cooked beans benefit from a smoked **ham hock** or a **ham bone** with some meat and fat on it. I wouldn't waste these on cooking a single can of beans - do at least **2 cans** if you have a hock or bone. Put the hock or bone in a pot and cover with water. Simmer it covered for at least an hour by itself. Remove it and save the water. You want to use the flavored water for cooking the beans. Cook the onion (Step2) in a little oil. Add the ham, ham liquid and beans to the pot. Add any needed water to just cover the beans. Add salt and pepper – a teaspoon of each. Cover and cook for at least 1-1/2 hours. Remove cover for the last 1/2 hour. Add 2 tablespoons of butter. **Taste for salt** at this point.

Recipe for 1 can of beans.

1. If you have a nice chunk of **leftover ham**, just dice up 1/3 cup with its fat and fry it in a pot until it starts to brown **or** if you don't have ham available you can dice up 1 or 2 strips of **bacon or** use a tablespoon of **bacon fat** if you have it. Fry the bacon until almost crisp in your saucepan. Don't want to use bacon or bacon fat, use some oil and go to the next step.

2. Add 1/3 cup chopped onion to the cooked ham or bacon and/or fat or oil add sauté it until translucent and it begins to brown. This gives the beans extra flavor.

3. Pour in a cup of water, wait a few seconds and scrape the bottom of the pan. This will deglaze the pan and bring up the flavorful browned bits. Add your beans and a teaspoon of salt and pepper. Add just enough water to cover them.

4. Simmer covered for 1-1/2 hours. (see NOTE below.) Remove cover and continue to simmer for the last 1/2 hour and add 2 tablespoons of butter. **Taste for salt** at this point. This is also the point where people add canned new potatoes or some unpeeled, small new potatoes cut in half. Be sure to submerged them in the liquid - stir them into the bottom.

NOTE: I have found that if you just bring your beans to a boil, cover and turn off the heat and let them sit for an hour or two they will have even more flavor. Then just cook them for about 1/2 hour to finish.

*TIP: I also like to add **tomatoes** sometimes – it adds a nice flavor. You can add some fresh chopped tomatoes or 1/2 can diced tomatoes (drained) at the beginning when you add the beans to the pot.*

OTHER VEGETABLES

Some common vegetables and ways to prepare them...

CARROTS

Carrots provide double duty. Not only are they eaten alone as a vegetable, but they are often used as part of a *mirepoix* - a mixture of celery, carrots and onions – to add flavor to other dishes.

Avoid buying those mini-carrots or pre-sliced or pre-shredded carrots. They are never very fresh. Their flavor is somewhat compromised. It only takes a minute to peel and chop or cut some carrots.

If your bagged carrots start to go limp, fill the bag with water. Most bags have holes, so let the water drain out. If there are no holes empty the water from the bag and seal it. This will bring them back to life. You could also cut them in half and put them in a container filled with water. Empty the water the next day.

Carrots can be boiled, steamed, microwaved or roasted in the oven. Roasting (at 400°F) always brings out the most flavor because it caramelizes the natural sugars in the vegetable. If you roast carrots they need little dressing, maybe a little butter.

If you steam or boil carrots you can drain off the water and add a tablespoon or two (depending on serving size) any of the following and sauté them for a few minutes.

- butter
- Red Pepper jelly for spicy carrots
- orange marmalade
- mix with some cooked peas ("peas and carrots")
- add fresh parsley

GLAZED CARROTS:
(2 servings)

1 cup carrots, peeled and sliced in 1/4 inch rounds
1 packed tablespoon of brown sugar
1 tablespoon butter
1/4 cup low sodium chicken broth
1/4 cup water
1/4 teaspoon salt
1/2 teaspoon lemon juice
1 teaspoon fresh minced parsley

Add the brown sugar, butter, broth, water and salt to a small heavy skillet and stir until the sugar is dissolved. Add carrots and simmer covered just until tender — 5 minutes. Remove carrots to a bowl and boil the liquid until it reduces to a syrup. Add carrots back to skillet and cook on low heat until carrots are warmed through and coated with the glaze. Stir in lemon juice and parsley.

PEAS

Today, the best way to buy peas is frozen. There is no reason to buy canned peas which have become too soft in the can. Fresh peas are great, but the downside, of course, is getting them out of their pods.

Peas are usually steamed or boiled. If adding peas to a casserole you don't need to cook them first. Just thaw frozen peas by just letting them sit a few minutes in hot tap water.

- Mix with carrots.

- Mix with snow pea pods. Thaw peas. Add them and snow pea pods to a lightly oiled or buttered skillet on medium heat and sauté for 3 minutes. No longer or the pea pods go limp.

- Sauté some sliced fresh mushrooms and thinly sliced celery in a little butter until the mushrooms are brown. Toss in some thawed peas, add a bit of salt and pepper and warm through.

The English like their **"mushy peas."** It certainly makes them easier to eat. Just cook the peas until tender. Drain, add a little butter, salt and pepper (and a few finely chopped mint leaves if you like) and use a potato masher to "mush" them up.

LIMA BEANS

Lima beans, also called butter beans, are one of my favorite beans. Unfortunately, you rarely see

them on menus. Frozen limas are your best bet, not canned. Two varieties are common — Fordhooks (larger beans) and baby limas. If you buy fresh pods and shell them they will take about 30 minutes to cook. Frozen take about 10 minutes.

Limas are steamed or boiled in salted water. If using in a recipe that requires baking they are usually cooked first.
- Limas are typically simply dressed with butter, but be creative!

- You can boil them in chicken stock for added flavor.

- After boiling/steaming sauté them in a little oil or butter with some finely chopped onion of bell pepper for a few minutes.

SUCCOTASH

Boil some lima beans and corn together. Dress with butter.

CORN

Avoid canned corn. Buy frozen. It retains all of its freshness. You can also buy ears of corn and cut off the kernels or eat it right off the cob.

FRIED CORN

Use either corn cut off the cob or frozen corn. Put it in a medium heat skillet with some butter or oil. Stir it often until tender and just beginning to brown a little. Add salt and pepper.

SPANISH CORN

Fry the corn as above with some chopped bell pepper and onion and mild green chiles.

BEANS

Beans are a legume – plants that bear their seeds or fruit in pods. Typically they are low in fat and high in protein and fiber. Yes, they are

high in carbohydrates (starch), but they are complex carbohydrates – the good kind. Canned varieties are higher in starch.

Today, most people buy their beans in a can or frozen because it takes a while to cook beans. Depending on the type it can take anywhere from 30 minutes to a few hours. The most common beans you find in the market are navy, red, pinto, kidney, white and black.

Beans are good eaten by themselves with a little seasoning or added to other dishes. If fresh they are always boiled.

STOVE-TOP "BAKED" BEANS:

Yes, you can buy baked beans "ready" to heat and eat, but it's easy to make your own. The beans will have more texture, too. Typically they are baked (duh), but when cooking for yourself it seems a lot of time and work to heat up an oven. This recipe uses plain beans, but you can use a canned baked beans. If you do, rinse the beans to remove the sauce because you are making your own.

(2 servings)
1 can of navy, pinto, black beans or even baby lima beans will work
2 strips of bacon chopped
1/8 cup brown sugar
1 small can tomato sauce or 1/4 cup of your favorite BBQ sauce
1/4 cup diced onion
1/2 tablespoon cider vinegar
1/4 cup water
1 teaspoon Worcestershire sauce
(optional) 1/8 cup diced green pepper
(optional) 1 tablespoon of molasses

In a medium saucepan brown the chopped bacon. Add the rest of the ingredients. If too thick add some water to thin so they will simmer. Taste the mixture. Too sweet - add a little vinegar, too sour - add a little brown sugar. Add some chili powder if you like a smoky flavor. Simmer for 20 to 30 minutes.

SQUASH

There are many types of squash, but we are most familiar with the green zucchini squash, the yellow squash, butternut and acorn squash.

Zucchini and yellow squash have seeds, but they are edible along with the flesh and skin. They are often simply sliced and sautéed in a pan with a little butter or oil and salt and pepper for a few minutes or chopped up or pureed and baked in a casserole type of dish.

Acorn and butternut squash are similar to melons in that they have a cavity of seeds that must be removed for cooking. They are delicious and a bit sweet. These squashes are usually roasted in some fashion to bring out their sugars. **Butternut squash** is normally peeled and the flesh is cut into cubes and roasted. **Acorn squash** can be halved, seeds removed, the cavity filled with a liquid mixture and then roasted.

ROASTED ACORN SQUASH
(serves 2)

1 Acorn squash cut in half side-to-side (not top to bottom). To make each half sit flat you might need to cut a little off each end.
2 tablespoons softened butter
2 tablespoons brown sugar
2 tablespoon maple syrup
Salt and pepper

Preheat oven to 400°F. Scoop out the seeds and pulp from the cavity and discard. Mix the butter, syrup, brown sugar, a little salt and pepper together in a small bowl. Using a pastry brush, lather the cavity and top with the mixture. Place them on a baking sheet in the preheated oven and bake 45-60 minutes until tender.

ROASTED BUTTERNUT SQUASH
(serves 4-6)

A butternut makes a lot of food. You can freeze leftovers and use them for a soup. (Thaw, add to blender with some chicken broth and puree. Put in a saucepan, add some milk or cream and a little nutmeg.)

1 large butternut squash (about 3 pounds), peeled, seeded and cut into one inch cubes
2 tablespoons olive oil
2 teaspoons salt
1 teaspoon black pepper
2 tablespoons brown sugar or honey
1 teaspoon cinnamon

Preheat oven to 425°F. Place the squash cubes on a roasting pan, drizzle with the oil, add salt, pepper, sugar and cinnamon and toss to coat. Spread the cubes out evenly in a single layer on a non-stick sheet pan. Roast for 30-45 minutes until slightly browned and tender, turning over with a spatula once during roasting.

ONIONS

Onions are typically used to add flavor to other dishes, but a baked, roasted or grilled onion is a tasty serving all by itself. I like an onion with a

steak or any cut of beef. As onions brown their natural sugars come out and they become sweet.

BAKED ONIONS:
Peel an onion, cut a little off each end, then cut it in half. Place the halves on a piece of foil large enough to wrap the onion, place a small pat of butter on the top and add a little salt and pepper. Bring the foil up the sides to create a basket leaving the top exposed. Bake at 425°F for 20-30 minutes until tender. (Test with a knife.)

GRILLED ONIONS:
Prepare as above, but completely wrap the onion in the foil. Put on the grill where they are not over direct heat or put them on a high grill shelf. Depending on size, they will take 20 or so minutes. Just pierce the foil and test for doneness.

BEETS

There is only one way I like beets — cold. Below is a simple recipe for pickled beets, nicely sweet and sour. Don't worry, you won't have to mess with cooking fresh beets — you will use canned.

(*Pickled beets are very delicious on a salad of spinach or baby greens with some crumbled blue cheese or goat cheese and some pecans or walnuts and dressed with a raspberry vinaigrette.*)

PICKLED BEETS

(2 or 3 servings as a side dish)
1, 14 ounce can of sliced beets drained
1/2 cup water
1/2 cup cider vinegar
2 teaspoons celery seed
1 tablespoon sugar
1/2 cup sliced onion (1/8 inch rounds cut into fourths)

Put the vinegar and sugar in a bowl and stir to dissolve the sugar. Add the water and taste. You want a sweet/sour balance. Add more sugar as needed. Add rest of ingredients and chill for several hours.

SPINACH

None of us eat enough spinach and it's so good for us. When you cook **fresh spinach** it reduces in volume greatly. A bag of spinach or head will look almost like nothing once heated and all it's water is released. The tough stems must also be removed before cooking.

I usually eat fresh spinach raw in a salad, preferring the smaller and more tender baby spinach

which doesn't need it's stems removed. Baby spinach is usually found in a bag or plastic container.

I use **frozen chopped spinach** for making a spinach casserole or creamed spinach. But **frozen spinach must be thawed and squeezed over and over** to remove its water or casseroles will be watery.

STOVE-TOP SPINACH

(2-3 servings)
1 box of frozen spinach thawed and squeezed dry.
2 strips of bacon
3 tablespoons finely chopped onion
1/2 tablespoon lemon zest
salt and pepper

Fry bacon and set aside to drain. Reserve 2 tablespoons of bacon fat in the pan. Add onions and sauté until tender - a few minutes. Add spinach to the pan with crumbled bacon, lemon zest and a little salt and pepper. Mix and heat through for 5 minutes.

APPENDIX

SAFE THAWING AND DEFROSTING METHODS

Uh, oh! You're home and forgot to thaw something for dinner. You grab a package of meat or chicken and use hot water to thaw it fast. But is this safe? What if you remembered to take food out of the freezer, but forgot and left the package on the counter all day while you were at work?

Neither of these situations is considered safe, and these methods of thawing may lead to foodborne illness. Raw or cooked meat, poultry or egg products, as any perishable foods, must be kept at a safe temperature during "the big thaw." They are safe indefinitely while frozen. However, as soon as they begin to thaw and become warmer than 40°F, bacteria that may have been present before freezing can begin to multiply.

Perishable foods should **never be thawed on the counter,** or **in hot water** and must **not be left at room temperature for more than two hours.** Also, never thaw foods in a garage, basement, car, dishwasher or plastic garbage bag; out on the kitchen counter, outdoors or on the porch. These methods can leave your foods unsafe to eat.

Even though the center of the package may still be frozen as it thaws on the counter, the outer layer of the food could be in the "Danger Zone," between 40° and 140°F – temperatures where bacteria multiply rapidly.

When thawing frozen food, it's best to plan ahead and thaw in the refrigerator where it will remain at a safe, constant temperature - at 40°F or below. There are three safe ways to thaw food: in the refrigerator, in cold water, and in the microwave.

REFRIGERATOR THAWING

Planning ahead is the key to this method because of the lengthy time involved. A large frozen item like a turkey requires at least a day (24 hours) for every 5 pounds of weight. Even small amounts of frozen food — such as a pound of ground meat or boneless chicken breasts — require a full day to thaw. When thawing foods in the refrigerator, there are variables to take into account.

• Some areas of the appliance may keep food colder than other areas.

• Food will take longer to thaw in a refrigerator set at 35°F than one set at 40°F.

After thawing in the refrigerator, items such as ground meat, stew meat, poultry, seafood, should remain safe and good quality for an additional day or two before cooking; red meat cuts (such as beef, pork or lamb roasts, chops and steaks) 3 to 5 days. Food thawed in the refrigerator can be refrozen without cooking, although there may be some loss of quality.

COLD WATER THAWING

This method is faster than refrigerator thawing but requires more attention. The food must be in a leak-proof package or plastic bag. If the bag leaks, bacteria from the air or surrounding environment could be introduced into the food. Also, the meat tissue may absorb water, resulting in a watery product. The bag should be submerged in cold tap water, changing the water every 30 minutes so it continues to thaw. Small packages of meat, poultry or seafood – about a pound – may thaw in an hour or less. A 3 to 4 pound package may take 2 to 3 hours. For whole turkeys, estimate about 30 minutes per pound. If thawed completely, the food must be cooked immediately. Foods thawed by the cold water method should be cooked before refreezing.

MICROWAVE THAWING

When thawing food in a microwave, plan to cook it immediately after thawing because some areas of the food may become warm and begin to cook during the thawing process (bringing the food to "Danger Zone" temperatures). Holding partially cooked food is not recommended because any bacteria present wouldn't have been destroyed and, indeed, the food may have reached optimal temperatures for bacteria to grow. After thawing in the microwave, always cook immediately after, whether microwave cooking, by conventional oven, or grilling. Foods thawed in the microwave should be cooked before refreezing.

COOKING WITHOUT THAWING

When there is not enough time to thaw frozen foods, or you're simply in a hurry, just remember: it is safe to cook foods from the frozen state. The cooking will take approximately 50% longer than the recommended time for fully thawed or fresh meat and poultry.

COOKING TIME / TEMPERATURE CHART

The chart is based on **resting times** - so allow meat to rest as described below after cooking. This not only allows the meat to come to the right temperature it also allows the meat juices to redistribute and keep the meat moist and juice.

After desired cooking temperature is reached, remove meat from heat source and **let stand 10 to 15 minutes before carving** (you may cover it with foil to prevent heat loss). The amount of time required for resting varies with the size of the cut of your meat. During this resting time, the meat continues to cook (meat temperature internally will rise 5 to 20 degrees after it is removed from the heat source) and the juices redistribute.

Cooking thermometers take the guesswork out of cooking, as they measures the internal temperature of your cooked meat, poultry, seafood, baked goods, and/or any casseroles, to assure that a safe temperature has been reached, harmful bacteria have been destroyed, and your food is cook perfectly. Always follow internal cooking temperatures to be safe!

A cooking or meat thermometer should not be a "sometime thing." A cooking thermometer can be used for all foods, not just meat. It measures the internal temperature of your cooked meat, poultry, seafood, breads, baked goods, and/or casseroles to assure that a safe temperature has been reached and that harmful bacteria (like certain strains of Salmonella and E. Coli) have been destroyed.

Foods are properly cooked only when they are heated at a high enough temperature to kill harmful bacteria that cause food-borne illness. Use it every time you prepare foods like beef, pork, poultry, roasts, hams, casseroles, meat loaves, egg dishes, and even your baked goods. **If you don't regularly use a thermometer, you should get into the habit of using one.**

According to the U.S. Department of Agriculture, internal temperature is the only way to gauge whether food is sufficiently cooked. USDA research reveals that the "color test" can give consumers misleading information about the safety of the foods they are preparing, since cooked color varies considerably. For example, freezing and thawing may influence a meat's tendency to brown prematurely.

USING A MEAT THERMOMETER

Some thermometers are instant-read, others take 5 to 10 seconds to show the final temperature.

Whole chicken or turkey: insert probe in the inner thigh area near the breast, where the thigh connects to the breast, but not touching the bone. If you are not sure, make a cut between the thigh and breast. If the juices run clear it is done. If they run pink, it is not done.

Roasts: insert probe into the middle of the thickest part of the meat.

CHICKEN AND TURKEY

Whole Chicken: INTERNAL TEMP: 160 to 165°F.

  5 to 7 pounds at 350°F. 2 to 2-1/4 hours:

Dark Meat (thigh or leg pieces), INTERNAL TEMP: 165°F.

  4 to 8 ounces at 350°F, 40-50 minutes:

Chicken Breast halves - bone-in, INTERNAL TEMP: 165°F.

  6 to 8 ounces at 350°F, 35-45 minutes

Whole Turkey (unstuffed)

  8 -12 pounds at 325°F, 2-3/4 - 3 hours
  12 -14 pounds at 325°F, 3 - 3-3/4 hours
  14 -18 pounds at 325°F, 3-3/4 - 4-1/4hours

Let it rest for at least 20-30 minutes before carving. A 12 pound turkey can handle 60 to 90 minute resting time during which the temper-ature can rise 30 degrees if covered and not exposed to drafts.

Turkey Breast: INTERNAL TEMP: 165°F.

  4 - 6 pounds at 325°F., 1-1/2 - 2-1/4 hours
  6 - 8 pounds at 325°F., 2-1/4 - 3-1/4 hours

PORK

Pork Loin Roast, Crown Roast
Roast at 325°F, 20 minutes per pound
Let stand 5 minutes before slicing.

> Medium - 140 to 145°F. (pale pink center)
> Well Done - 160°F and above (uniformly
>   brown throughout)

Pork Tenderloin
Roast at 425°F, 45 minutes to 1 hour

> Pink Center - 130°F.
> Well Done - 160°F.

BEEF

Steaks: Always let steaks rest for at least 5 minutes so juices will re-absorb into meat.

> Rare: 120 - 125°F.
> Medium Rare: 130 - 135°F.
> Medium: 140 - 145°F.
> Medium Well: 150 - 155°F.
> Well Done: 160°F and above.

Brisket
> 165 - 175° F

Meatloaf
> 160 - 165° F

Rib Eye Roast (boneless) *Let stand 10-15 minutes before slicing.*
Roast at 350°F.

> **3 to 4 pounds**
> Medium Rare - 135°F. 1-1/2 to 2 hours
> Medium -150°F. 1-3/4 to 2 hours

> **4 to 6 pounds**
> Medium Rare - 135°F. 2 - 2-1/2 hours
> Medium -150°F.   2 - 2-3/4 hours

> **6 to 8 pounds**
> Medium Rare - 135°F.   2-1/2 - 2-3/4 hours
> Medium -150°F. 2-1/2 - 2-3/4 hours

Rib Roast (bone-in) *Let stand 15-20 minutes before slicing.*
Roast at 350°F.

> **4 to 6 pounds (2 ribs)**
> Medium Rare - 135°F. 1-1/2 to 2 hours
> Medium -150°F. 1-3/4 to 2 hours

> **6 to 8 pounds (2 to 4 ribs)**
> Medium Rare - 135°F. 2 - 2-1/2 hours
> Medium -150°F. 2 - 2-3/4 hours

> **8 to 10 pounds (4 to 5 ribs)**
> Medium Rare - 135°F. 2-1/2 - 2-3/4 hours
> Medium -150°F. 2-1/2 - 2-3/4 hours

Beef Tenderloin, *Let stand 10-15 minutes before slicing.*
Roast at 425°F.

> **2 to 3 pounds**
> Medium Rare - 135°F. 35-40 minutes
> Medium -150°F. 45-50 minutes

> **4 to 5 pounds**
> Medium Rare - 135°F. 50-60 minutes
> Medium -150°F. 60-70 minutes

Eye of Round Roast, *Let stand 15-20 minutes before slicing.*
Roast at 325°F.

> **2 to 3 pounds**
> Medium Rare - 135°F. 1-/12—1-3/4 hours
> Medium: 140 - 145°F.
> Medium Well: 150 - 155°F.
> Well Done: 160°F and above.

A WEEK OF SUPPERS

This is a list of possible meals for each day of the week divided by cooking times so you can decide how much time you have to prepare your meal. Each day uses a different main ingredient — Monday is beef-based dishes, Tuesday is chicken-based dishes, etc. All dishes are based on recipes in this book. You may have some of your own recipes you can pencil into the categories. Saturday and Sunday are left blank as you will likely eat out or maybe carry-out one day a week. These are your "exchange" days to switch out with another day. The list doesn't account for **leftovers** you might eat within the next day or two. **Soup and/or a sandwich** or **salad** is always a nice, light dinner option. Soup can also take the place of a salad, starch or vegetable with any entree or be a meal itself especially with some good bread. **A salad with some sliced grilled or pan-fried chicken** also makes a nice, light supper.

Side dishes are suggested as options that can be made in the same amount or less time than the entree, however some need to chill for an hour or more so if you are in a rush make them the night before or in the morning. <u>They are underlined</u>. See recipe for time.

You can always cook low and slow recipes the night before - throw it together after dinner, cook, refrigerate, and reheat a portion the next evening for dinner, refrigerate leftovers for another meal or freeze for another time.

BEEF MONDAY

30 minutes	**Hamburgers** • <u>slaw</u>, home fries
	Steak • baked potato (microwave), home fries, salad, fresh green beans, broccoli, cauliflower, asparagus
	Beef Stir-Fry (using round steak sliced in thin strips) • rice, <u>fried rice</u>
60 minutes	**Chili-Mac**
	Hamburger BBQ • <u>slaw</u>, home fries
	Meatloaf (longer depending on size) • mashed potatoes, green beans, corn
90 minutes	**Roast of Beef** • mashed potatoes, roasted potatoes, green vegetable
	Chili (but cooking longer is better)
3 hours or more (low-and-slow)	**Pot Roast** • mashed potatoes, green vegetable, carrots, peas
	Brisket • mashed potatoes or roasted potatoes, green vegetable, carrots, peas, Brussels sprouts
	Beef Stroganoff • egg noodles, green vegetable
	Chili
	Swiss Steak • mashed potatoes or buttered egg noodles, green vegetable
30 minutes	*with leftover Pot Roast:* Beef Stroganoff, Beef BBQ, Beef Enchiladas
	with leftover Chili: Chili-Mac
	with leftover Brisket or Roast of Beef: hot or cold roast beef sandwich, BBQ, Enchiladas, Stir-Fry
60 minutes	*with leftover Pot Roast or Roast of Beef:* Beef Pot Pie

CHICKEN TUESDAY

USING CHICKEN CUTLETS
(chicken cutlets or boneless/skinless breasts or thighs pounded thinly).

30 minutes

Chicken Marsala • mashed potatoes or rice pilaf (box) or buttered egg noodles, asparagus, broccoli, spinach, salad

Chicken Piccata • mashed potatoes or rice pilaf (box) or buttered egg noodles, asparagus, broccoli, spinach, salad

Chicken Parmesan • spaghetti, salad

Chicken Cordon Blue-ish • rice pilaf (box mix), salad, green vegetable

Chicken and Mushrooms • mashed potatoes or buttered egg noodles or rice, green vegetable, salad

Chicken Fingers • tater tots or home fries, slaw, potato salad, macaroni salad

Stir-Fry • rice or fried rice

with leftover Chicken from oven-fried, baked or roast chicken: Enchiladas, Stir Fry, Chicken and Dumplings

60 minutes

Enchiladas • beans and rice

with leftover Chicken from oven-fried, baked or roast chicken or Turkey: Pot Pie, Chicken (Turkey)Tetrazzini

USING CHICKEN PARTS
bone-in, skin-on breasts, thighs, legs, wings

60 minutes

Chicken Cacciatore • pasta, egg noodles, salad

Oven-Fried Chicken • mashed potatoes or slaw, rice with mushroom gravy (see oven-fried chicken recipe), lima beans, broccoli, cauliflower, peas and carrots, baked beans

Baked Chicken • mashed potatoes or rice pilaf, green vegetable, cranberry sauce

Chicken and Dumplings • peas and carrots or green vegetable

90 minutes

Chicken Tetrazzini • cranberry sauce, salad

Pot Pie • salad

USING BONELESS CHICKEN BREASTS OR THIGHS (skin on)

60 minutes

Chicken and Dumplings • peas and carrots or green vegetable

Chicken Cacciatore • pasta, egg noodles, salad

USING A WHOLE CHICKEN

90 minutes plus

Roast Chicken • mashed potatoes, rice pilaf, asparagus, Brussels sprouts, lima beans, green beans, broccoli, cauliflower, peas and carrots

PORK WEDNESDAY

30 minutes	**Pan-Fried Pork Chop or Pork Cutlets** • sweet potato or rice pilaf (box) or <u>fried rice</u>, fried apples, green vegetable **Pork Dijonaise** • sweet potato or home fries, green vegetable, salad **Smoked Sausage** • boiled and buttered potatoes or home fries, cooked cabbage, green vegetable
30 minutes	*with leftover Pork:* Pork BBQ using BBQ ribs meat or pork tenderloin Stir-Fry using pork tenderloin Enchiladas using pork tenderloin or loin roast
60 minutes	**Pork Tenderloin Roast** (*if marinating add at least 1 to 2 hours*) • baked potato or sweet potato or <u>fried rice</u>, green vegetable, Brussels sprouts, asparagus
90 minutes	**Pork Chops Creole** • egg noodles, green vegetable **Pork Loin Roast** • mashed potatoes or sweet potato or <u>fried rice</u>, green vegetable, Brussels sprouts, asparagus
3 hours plus	**BBQ Spare Ribs, Baby-Back Ribs or Country-Style Ribs** • <u>slaw</u>, <u>potato salad</u>, baked beans, green beans

PASTA THURSDAY

30 minutes	**Pasta with Olive Oil and Garlic** • salad, green vegetable unless you add a vegetable to the recipe as described, some good French bread **Pasta Primavera** • salad, some good French bread **Spaghetti alla Carbonara** • salad, some good French bread **Fettuccine Alfredo** • salad, asparagus, some good French bread **Thin Crust Pizza**
60 minutes	(*If you have a prepared or frozen marinara or meat sauce; 90 minutes to 2 hours if you make a quick marinara or meat sauce*) **Baked Ziti** • salad, some good French bread **Lasagna** • salad, some good French bread **Stuffed Shells** • salad, some good French bread
4 hours plus	**Spaghetti and Meatballs** • salad, some good French bread

SEAFOOD FRIDAY

30 minutes	**Pan-Fried, Baked, Broiled or Grilled Fish or Salmon** • rice pilaf (box), <u>fried rice</u>, <u>slaw</u>, buttered noodles, boiled and buttered potatoes, home fries, green vegetable, salad
	Quick Salmon Croquettes • home fries, pickled beets, slaw, green vegetable, salad,
	Shrimp Scampi • rice or spaghetti, green vegetable, salad
	Shrimp Creole • salad
60 minutes	**Crab Cakes** (*requires prep and chilling for at least 1 hour*) • <u>slaw</u>, buttered boiled potatoes or home fries, spanish or fried corn or succotash
3 hours plus	**Salmon Croquettes** (*requires prep and chilling for at least 3 hours*) • <u>pickled beets</u>, <u>slaw</u>

SATURDAY & SUNDAY

For these days pick something from another day of the week. Sunday is a good day to roast or oven-fry chicken, make a pot roast or pork roast or BBQ ribs if you have the time. If you would rather have something quick pick something else.

THINGS I KNOW HOW TO COOK

Make a list of recipes/foods you know how to cook here.

HERBS & SPICES

Herbs and spices give so much flavor to food. American cuisine tends to use less than other cultures. This list of the most commonly used herbs and spices gives you an idea of what these important elements add to recipes.

ALLSPICE tastes of cinnamon, cloves and nutmeg, but more pungent. Used in spice mixes or to flavor spice cakes and cookies, pies, BBQ sauce and corned beef.

BASIL is a highly aromatic herb with a robust clove and licorice flavor used both fresh and dried depending on the recipe. Used in pestos or shredded as a finishing touch on pasta dishes. Can be grown indoors.

BAY LEAF imparts a woodsy note to soups and sauces and is often used in braised meat dishes. Can be grown indoors.

CARAWAY is a nutty, licorice-flavored seed used in rye bread, cole slaw, cooked cabbage, sauerkraut, winter squashes and marinara sauces.

CAYENNE PEPPER is made from dried and ground red chili peppers. It adds a sweet heat to soups, braises and spice mixes. Use carefully - add by pinches.

CELERY SEED tastes like its name used in salads like potato salad and slaws.

CHIVE is a delicate herb with an onion and garlic taste. Best to use fresh as dried has little flavor at all. Used in cream soups and sauces with fish, cheese, eggs and as a garnish.

CILANTRO is a leafy herb that has a slight soapy flavor. Used a lot in International cuisines.

CINNAMON is a bark with a sweet, hot, earthy flavor used in both sweet and savory dishes. Comes as a powder or sticks.

CLOVES add sweetness and warmth. Usually used in baking, but can also be good with braised meat. Use sparingly.

CUMIN is smoky and earthy. Most often used in Southwestern, Mexican, North African, Middle Eastern, and Indian cuisines. Typically used in chili or as part of a chili powder mix or in BBQ rubs and sauces.

DILL comes ground, as seeds or fresh. Seeds are the most pungent. Used for pickling, to flavor fish and salmon, cucumbers, potatoes, egg dishes and used in sauces.

FENNEL SEED is a licorice flavored seed used in meat dishes, meatballs, marinara sauces.

GARLIC POWDER is made from dehydrated garlic cloves and can be used to give dishes a sweeter, more mellow garlic flavor.

GINGER can be bought as a ground powder or as a fresh root which has much more flavor. Peel and grate with a microplane. Has some bite and aroma. Used in marinades, Asian dishes, sweet baked goods

MARJORAM is floral and woodsy, a milder version of oregano.

MINT is a very versatile herb often paired with lamb, peas, potatoes and chocolate. Can be grown indoors.

NUTMEG is an earthy and pungent spice often used in baked goods or as a warming note to savory dishes. Best to buy whole seeds (size of a grape) and grate them fresh on a microplane.

OREGANO is a robust, somewhat earthy in flavor. Used in a lot of Mexican, Mediterranean and Italian dishes. Dried is usually preferred over fresh as it has a more intense the flavor. Can be grown indoors.

PAPRIKA and Smoked Paprika add a spicy, earthy note and red color with the smoked variety having a richer, smokey flavor. Used in stews and spice blends.

PARSLEY is a crisp, fresh herb that tastes a bit like celery. Italian flat leaf (stronger flavor) and curly are the main varieties. Used in just about anything; good for soups like chicken soup, usually added just at the end so the fresh flavor doesn't cook out. Also used in many pasta dishes just at the end or as a general food garnish. Can be grown indoors. Never use dried parsley!

ROSEMARY is strong and piney. Often used with pork, chicken, lamb, potatoes and grilled meats. Can overpower a dish so use carefully.

SAGE has a pine-like, musky flavor, more lemony and eucalyptus notes than rosemary. Found in a lot of northern Italian cooking and often used with chicken or pork dishes and in bread dressings.

TARRAGON has a strong anise flavor. Used in salads or used to flavor tomato dishes, seafood or eggs.

TURMERIC is often used more for its yellow color than its flavor (a substitute for saffron), but it has a mild, woodsy flavor.

THYME adds a pungent, woodsy, minty tea-like flavor; a bit like oregano. Used often with fish, poultry, tomatoes, potatoes. Can be grown indoors.

INDEX

Measurements

a pinch = slightly less than 1/4 teaspoon	8 ounces = 1 cup
a dash = a few drops	2 cups = 1 pint = 1/2 quart
3 teaspoons = 1 tablespoon	4 cups = 2 pints = 1 quart
2 tablespoons = 1/8 cup = 1 ounce	4 quarts = 1 gallon
4 tablespoons = 1/4 cup	
4 ounces = 1/2 cup	1 stick of butter is 1/4 pound of butter = 4 ounces of butter
16 ounces = 1 pound	
8 tablespoons = 1/2 cup = 4 ounces	2 sticks of butter is 1/2 pound of butter

Metric Conversions
Some of the basic metric system and celsius cooking conversions.

LIQUID or VOLUME MEASURES (approx.)	DRY or WEIGHT MEASURES (approx.) (flour, sugar, meats, fish)
1 teaspoon = 5 ml	1 ounce = 30 grams
1 tablespoon = 15 ml	2 ounces = 55 g
2 tablespoons = 30 ml	3 ounces = 85 g
1/4 cup = 60 ml	4 ounces = 125 g
1/2 cup = 125 ml	8 ounces = 240 g
1/3 cup = 80 ml	12 ounces = 375 g
2/3 cup = 160 ml	16 ounces (1 pound) = 454 g
3/4 cup = 177 ml	32 ounces = 907 g
1 cup = 237 ml	1 pound = 454 g
2 cups (1 pint) = 473 ml	2 pounds = 907 g
4 cups = 946 ml, .95 liter	
1 pint (2 cups) = 473 ml	**BUTTER:**
1 ounce = 30 ml	1 tablespoon = 14 g = 1/2 ounce
4 ounces = 120 ml	1/2 cup = 1 stick = 113 g
8 ounces (1 cup) = 237 ml	1 cup = 2 sticks = 227 g

Typical oven temperatures:	Internal meat temperatures:
200 F = 93 C	130 F = 55 C
250 F = 120 C	135 F = 57 C
275 F = 135 C	140 F = 60 C
300 F = 149 C	145 F = 63 C
325 F = 163 C	150 F = 66 C
350 F = 177 C	155 F = 68 C
375 F = 190 C	160 F = 71 C
400 F = 204.5 C	165 F = 74 C
425 F = 220 C	170 F = 77 C
450 F = 232 C	175 F = 80 C
500 F = 260 C	

CPSIA information can be obtained at www.ICGtesting.com
Printed in the USA
BVOW04s1109131215

430146BV00032B/857/P